SECOND ED

VOLUME 1

SECURING
THE FUTURE

BUILDING YOUR FIRM'S
SUCCESSION PLAN

14821V1-349

AICPA® PCPS

Bill Reeb, CPA/CITP, CGMA
Dom Cingoranelli, CPA, CGMA

Notice to Readers

Securing the Future, Volume 1: Building Your Firm's Succession Plan does not represent an official position of the American Institute of Certified Public Accountants, and it is distributed with the understanding that the author and publisher are not rendering legal, accounting, or other professional services in the publication. This book is intended to be an overview of the topics discussed within, and the author has made every attempt to verify the completeness and accuracy of the information herein. However, neither the author nor publisher can guarantee the applicability of the information found herein. If legal advice or other expert assistance is required, the services of a competent professional should be sought.

Publisher: Linda Prentice Cohen
Acquisitions Editor: Erin Valentine
Developmental Editor: Katie Hurst
Project Manager: Amy Sykes
Publishing Specialist: R. Ingrid Medina

Acknowledgments

First, we want to thank the PCPS Executive Committee for engaging us to do this project. George Willie (chair of the PCPS Executive Committee) provided strong leadership in the level of information covered in this manuscript as well insight into overall content, which will prove to meet the needs of the profession.

We also want to thank the many firms that participated in the 2012 PCPS/Succession Institute Succession Planning Survey (our survey update).

Finally, we would like to thank Erin Valentine, our editor, for putting up with us, riding herd on us, and making sure this product was the best it could be. She was easy to work with and did a great job of balancing being flexible and forceful in organizing, simplifying, and improving our work.

The following AICPA/PCPS staff are people that we specifically want to name who supported us in this project:

PCPS Staff Members

Mark Koziel   Natasha Schamberger

AICPA Editorial and Production

Erin Valentine, Acquisitions Editor   Annmarie Piacentino, Copy Editor

Kathleen Hurst, Developmental Editor   Amy Sykes, Project Manager

The following are members of the PCPS Executive Committee who provided direction for and supported this book.

Cheryl Burke
DiCicco, Gulman & Company, LLP
Woburn, Massachusetts

Joseph Falbo, CPA, CGMA
Trconi Segarra & Associates, LLP
Williamsville, New York

Jason Deshayes, CPA
Butler & Company, CPAs
Albuquerque, New Mexico

Chris Farmand, CPA, CITP
Chris Farmand + Company
Jacksonville, Florida

Loretta Doon, CPA
California Society of CPAs
San Mateo, California

Melody Feniks, CPA, CGMA
Feniks & Company, LLC
Fairbanks, Alaska

Charles Fredrick, CPA
FredrickZink & Associates, CPAs
Durgano, Colorado

Robert Goldfarb, CPA, CFP, CGMA, PFS,
CFE, DABFE, DABFA
Janover LLC
Garden City, New York

Carter Heim, CPA, CFF, CGMA, MST
HeimLantz
Annapolis, Maryland

Karen Kerber, CPA, CITP, CGMA
Kerber, Rose & Associates, S.C.
Shawano, Wisconsin

Alexandra Kessler, CPA, CGMA
Aronson LLC
Rockville, Maryland

Joel Olbricht, CPA
Olbricht Storniolo Group LLC
Hampstead, New Hampshire

Scot Phillips, CPA
Eide Bailly, LLP
Boise, Idaho

Jacquelyn Tracy, CPA, CGMA
Mandel & Tracy, LLC
Providence, Rhode Island

James Walker, CPA
Cherry Bekaert LLP
Richmond, Virginia

George Willie, CPA, PFF, CGFM, CGMA
Bert Smith & Co.
Washington, District of Columbia

About the Authors

Bill Reeb

Bill has been consulting for over three decades to all sizes of businesses, from mom and pop operations to Fortune 100 companies. Prior to his life as a CPA, he worked for IBM in sales back in the late '70s. As an entrepreneur, Bill has founded seven small businesses, from retail to software development to advisory work.

An award-winning public speaker, Bill lectures throughout the U.S. and Canada to thousands of executives and CPAs each year. As an award-winning author, Bill is internationally published, with numerous magazines, journals, newspapers, and books to his credit. Besides *Securing the Future*, Bill and his partner Dom Cingoranelli have also authored *Becoming a Trusted Business Advisor: How to Add Value, Improve Client Loyalty, and Increase Profits*. In addition, Bill has a new book out on managing your life titled *The Overachiever's Guide to Getting Unstuck: Replan, Reprioritize, Reaffirm*.

Bill is an active volunteer within his profession, having served in many leadership roles in both the state and national organizations. He is an avid golfer and skier, but spends the majority of his free time learning and teaching martial arts.

Dom Cingoranelli

Dom's consulting experience over the last three decades includes organizational development work for CPA firms and associations, as well as on construction projects for the Big Three auto makers; for regional, national, and international contractors; and for organizations in a variety of other industries. He has performed strategy consulting and planning; process improvement studies; management consulting, training, and development; team building; coaching; and group process facilitation for a variety of groups.

He co-authored *Securing the Future* and *Becoming a Trusted Business Advisor: How to Add Value, Improve Client Loyalty, and Increase*

Profits, as well as the AICPA PCPS Succession Resource Center and Trusted Business Advisor Resource Center. Dom has also written numerous articles and CPE offerings on executive recruiting, performance management, leadership, planning, and organizational culture. He speaks frequently on management and consulting topics throughout the country.

When he is not working, you may find Dom doing volunteer work at his church, tying flies, fly fishing, or touring on his Gold Wing.

CONTENTS

Chapter 1: Why Now?

Why Does This Matter, and Why Now?

Why now, indeed! Why would anyone care now about the topic of succession management? Consider the AICPA Private Company Practice Section (PCPS) top issues survey for the last 6 years. Succession ranked in the top 5 issues for each of those surveys for firms with 21 or more professionals (succession management showed up as issue 3, issue 5, and most recently as issue 4 of their top concerns). Of course, we're biased, but we believe one would have to have been living in a cave for the last 5 years not to be aware of the importance of the succession management topic to our profession. Although an individual firm reading this might not consider succession a top priority, largely due to some basic demographic facts of life, almost 80 percent of multiowner firms responding to the most recent PCPS/Succession Institute Succession Survey felt like succession management would be a significant issue for them in the next 10 years. Considering that less than 10 percent of sole proprietors and solo practitioners in that same survey even have a practice continuation agreement, that group clearly isn't ready for succession, either.

To put this in perspective, baby boomers, who were born and grew up after World War II (1946–1964), make up a large portion of the working U.S. population. A myriad of issues has come with the aging of this group, not the least of which is dealing with the exit strategies of business owners, together with all the related issues of retirement and overall financial planning for retirement. And it's not going to get any better in the near future—baby boomers currently account for more than 1 in 4 Americans.[1] At the same time, the subsequent generations are smaller in size than the boomer generation, resulting in concerns about who is even available to replace exiting boomers across all segments, industries, and professions. And when you consider "The U.S. Census Report 65+ in the United States: 2005," which estimated a total of 36 million people 65 years of age or over in 2003, and projects for that same category 72 million in 2030 and 87 million in 2050, it is easy to see why demographers are calling this the "silver tsunami." In a speech at a recent AICPA Council meeting, Dr. James H. Johnson, Jr., of the University of North Carolina at Chapel Hill, noted that over 8,000 people per day are turning 65 in the United States (or someone is turning 65 about every 6 seconds), and it is expected that this trend will continue for the next 2 decades. Regardless of your profession or

---

[1] See www.bbhq.com/bomrstat.htm and http://seniors.lovetoknow.com/Baby_Boomer_Statistics.

industry, if succession management is not a near-term issue for you to address right now (based on demographics alone), it will likely be one for you to address soon.

Given this, it should be no surprise that we believe that all organizations need to plan for succession, whether they are nonprofit or for-profit in nature, and whether they are in the business of selling goods or time or expertise. This text and its companion field guide, *Securing the Future, Volume 2: Implementing Your Firm's Succession Plan*, focus on succession planning for public accounting and consulting firms, but the techniques and principles we discuss are applicable to virtually all personal service businesses and many other organizations, as well.

We created this two-book series because we wanted one volume to cover fundamental succession and management concepts, so that every partner, as well as those in key leadership roles throughout the firm, could quickly and easily review the opportunities and obstacles the succession process creates. In this book, we keep the focus of the material at 10,000 feet—far enough away that we don't get into the implementation minutiae, but close enough that the discussion points will resonate both at an organizational and a personal level. By getting everyone who will be involved in the decision making regarding your firm's succession approach to read this, you should not only be able to more quickly discuss the various issues, opportunities, and ramifications of whatever decisions your firm makes, but also be able to cover them in a less personal manner (meaning the issues are raised as best practice ideas rather than someone's personal preference or perceived entitlement). We created the second volume, *Implementing Your Firm's Succession Plan*, for those who are charged with implementing the plan once your firm decides what that plan is going to be. This second book, a companion to this volume, delves into far more detail, providing strategies, tactics, action plans, and tools to help you complete each step in your plan.

Succession planning for personal service businesses, like CPA firms, can be more difficult than succession planning for other types of organizations. This is because a personal service business, by its very nature, depends on good, strong relationships with clients. By its nature, a personal service business is much more likely to be identified with the individual partner or partners, rather than with the firm itself; and the smaller the CPA firm and its clients, the more likely this will be the case. When you consider that out of some 44,000 CPA firms in the United States, 40,000 of those firms have 10 professionals or fewer, which translates to a significant number of small businesses that would identify with their specific CPA rather than the firm in which that CPA works. The more an organization can create an institutional identity and loyalty to that organization's brand, the easier it is for changes to occur in ownership and management without affecting viability or future success. But real institutional identity and brand loyalty rarely occur in the smaller professional service organizations, creating greater risk in long-term viability when key partners transition out of the business. This is typically exacerbated even more when you consider how many small firms operate as solo practices where there are currently *no* candidates on board for internal succession.

Most professional service organizations have quite a bit of work to do to get ready for succession. Regardless of size, there are options available, and this book was written to help every firm think through its options and outline a plan to move forward.

Succession planning, and doing business in general, is not made any easier by the fact that we live and work in a dynamic, competitive environment. Every organization must deal with competitive threats, some of which the organization may not even be aware of until the threats are catastrophic in size and nature. Consider the example of Kodak and the impact of digital photography on its business. For years, it had a lock on the market for film and film processing, but times have changed. There are many other examples, and each organization is subject to its own unique threats and challenges coming from expected, and unexpected, quarters. Depending on the business you're in and the market segments you serve, your organization will be affected favorably or unfavorably by trends in areas such as the following:

- Demographics
- Technology
- Regulation and legislation
- Your clients' or customers' market segments

We are not dedicating space in this manuscript to the details of these various trends because you most likely have been staying updated through professional and trade associations that monitor and report on them continually. If you are not staying updated, check with your professional or industry associations for more specifics.[2] Suffice it to say there are many external forces you need to observe to successfully compete over the long term, not to mention deal with effective succession management. This is as true for CPA firms of all sizes as it is for any other organization.

As well, there are many moving parts, processes, and policies within an organization involved in making succession happen successfully. Unfortunately, many CPA firm owners haven't given these varied elements adequate consideration, if any, in their succession planning to date. This book will cover what we perceive as the most critical of those moving parts and how they are integrated with each other. We will also discuss why it is so important, as you work through this process, to recognize that each time you frame up one of those moving parts, you must understand that your current solution only stands as a placeholder until you have identified the entire plan. With each step you take toward completion of the process, more light may be shed on the adequacy or suitability of previous decisions, resulting in the need to further tweak or redefine an earlier step in your process.

In addition to the pressure of dealing with the business and economic aspects of exit strategies and retirement planning, there is also the psychological issue of ultimately needing to face our mortality, our health, our mental faculties, and the fact that many people within our profession have allowed their work to become almost their entire identity, all of which add a great deal of complexity to addressing succession management. Over the years, we are bombarded by stories about an untimely death or other tragic incident that has cut a productive life short. Unfortunately, more and more, we can tell our own sad stories regarding the unexpected death or disability of our friends and acquaintances. Although this barrage of information heightens our awareness of how quickly life can change, it is still surprising how many of us try to ignore it and, therefore, don't prepare for the possibility that this kind of tragedy can happen to us. We believe *we* will have plenty of time to see, plan for, and react to any major changes coming into view on our horizon, even if others didn't or won't. This is not just about dying and making sure we have made arrangements for our estates to be paid out under a buy-sell agreement because that part is easy. We also need to address partial or full disability, how we are going to deal with a partner's declining mental capacity, or what we are going to do to make sure partners retire at an appropriate time to allow future leadership to flourish.

---

[2] For example, CPA firms have access to a wealth of information through the AICPA, its Private Company Practice Section, and their state CPA association or society.

Unfortunately, in the work we do with CPA firms and other organizations around the country, especially given the graying of the baby boomer generation, we increasingly encounter abrupt, debilitating health, mental, and performance issues that are devastating organizations. Many CPA firm partners perceive this to be more of a personal issue than an organizational concern. All too often, they don't look at their organizations as entities that need to be protected. Although CPAs may obtain insurance (life, disability, or both), often, they stop there and don't spend the time necessary to plan for extending the life of the business to ensure that it remains a going concern for the surviving partners, employees, and clients or customers.

Over the years, in partnership with PCPS,[3] we've conducted a variety of succession-planning surveys specifically for the CPA profession. It may surprise readers to know that over the last 12 years, although we've seen some improvements in succession management practices at CPA firms, in many cases, there is a tremendous amount of room for improvement. For example, even using a liberal definition of a *succession plan*, less than half of the multi-owner firms in our last survey claimed they have one. Of those who reported that they did have a plan, only about 50 percent of those plans are firmed up and finalized. Surveying the anecdotal evidence we have acquired through speaking and working with firms all over the United States and Canada, it is rare to find a plan robust enough to adequately manage a near-seamless transition from the retiring to the incoming generation of leaders even among those firms that claim they have a fully functioning succession plan. To most firms, a succession plan is just the following:

- A schedule by age of the partners.
- An estimate about who might decide to leave when (but nothing more than that because no one has truly committed to going, and virtually everyone could go).
- A schedule outlining what the firm thinks it will owe each partner based on when the group guesses they are leaving.
- An analysis about whether the firm's cash flow can afford the retirement payments.
- Some list of people who might be named partners in the future.
- A list of clients who need to be transitioned to someone.

Although these are issues that need to be identified and addressed, they are just the tip of the iceberg. As part of our discussion in the remainder of this chapter, we will cover the high level component parts of a succession plan that can make a difference.

Why CPAs Don't Develop Successors As They Should

CPAs can cite a litany of reasons for not actively grooming their successors and developing robust succession plans. Such reasons often include statements similar to the following:

- I don't have time—other business demands preclude it at this time.
- I have plenty of people here who might be candidates, but there are no legitimate candidates now. I will watch to see who develops, if anyone develops.

---

[3] See www.aicpa.org/InterestAreas/PrivateCompaniesPracticeSection/StrategyPlanning/center/ DownloadableDocuments/SuccessionSurveyMultiComm.pdf for the most recent succession planning report.

- We have a number of partners in our organization, but they are technicians and not suitable for leading this firm.
- I am not planning on retiring for another 5–10 years, so there is no reason to pursue this just yet.
- I plan on selling the firm to another CPA firm because I don't have the leadership talent necessary to pay me off.
- I plan on selling the firm to another CPA firm because my partners will run this business into the ground once I leave, and I have no assurance that I will ever see my retirement paid in full.
- I plan on working until I don't want to do this anymore, and at that time, I will consider my options.
- I am taking all the money out each year, and when it comes time to retire, I will get what I can and just close up shop. In other words, I just make the money now, rather than make it later.
- My son or daughter will work here for a while and step into the position, so I don't need to worry about it now.

Many unstated reasons for not developing successors might include the following:

- I am struggling with my own mortality (recognizing it is time to retire) or identity (as a senior partner, I may not have developed any significant outside interests and don't have a clear idea of what I will do with my time if I retire, so I don't want to think about it).
- The need for control—I do not want to give up the authority required to help my people develop decision-making skills.
- I believe it takes time and money out of my pocket to develop talent. Therefore, it is a better investment to make do with what I have and focus on being as efficient and as profitable as I can be right now. When the time comes for retiring, I will see who is out there to take over the firm.
- I don't want to develop some young partner to take over because the younger partner may get tired of waiting and try to force me out before I want to leave.
- I enjoy being the go-to person and running the firm my way. I prefer to be needed and surround myself with people who make my life easier, rather than developing successors who can do what I do.

It doesn't really matter what a person's reasons are for not developing successors or creating a succession plan. What matters is that for the most part, these reasons are simply excuses for putting it off. Ignoring the problem will *not* make it go away. However, ignoring the problem *will* diminish the number and quality of options available to you over time. More options generally lead to more success and satisfaction with the outcomes, especially when it comes to exit strategies and succession planning.

We will look at two different types of succession planning: crisis succession planning and orderly succession planning.

Crisis Succession Planning

This is the planning an organization needs to conduct in order to prepare for an unexpected vacancy in a key position resulting from a sudden departure, death, or disability. Unfortunately, this type of planning is usually done at the time of the incident rather than as advance preparation. Partner groups, led by the managing partner, should periodically review their firms' key positions and look at who is available to fill in—at least temporarily—for the incumbent in the case of an unplanned vacancy. In addition, the crisis succession planning process focuses on developing "seconds," or replacements, for all key positions.

In addition to identifying potential candidates to fill key positions, an organization should ensure that job descriptions and expected competencies of the key positions are updated periodically. Consider documenting key clients and other external contacts of the incumbent, both of which are critical for anyone stepping in to carry out this person's duties. Is that information updated periodically, as well? Does anyone else in the firm know where to find this documentation if it is needed? Does anyone else in the firm actually know any of these people?

The point is that crisis succession planning, which, in our experience, is the type of advance planning least often performed by CPA firms, should outline processes to constantly capture the necessary information and require that almost every position, especially key positions, have "seconds" identified and in the process of being groomed. Although this sounds like a negative and morbid approach, developing this kind of organizational chart and establishing career paths for your people is simply good personnel management.

Orderly Succession Planning

This is the type of planning that probably comes to mind for most CPA firm partners, unless they have recently encountered a crisis in a key position. However, as we mentioned previously, it entails more than simply working out buy-sell agreements and finding ways and means to fund them. *Orderly succession planning* refers to, in the broadest sense, the people and process aspects of succession planning. On one end of the spectrum, the partner group, led by the managing partner, should be doing the following:

- *Identifying future leaders.* Who among the current staff and managers show some entrepreneurial promise (this is about more than just cranking out charge hours)?
- *Determining future skills and competencies needed among the leadership group.* What specific competencies and observable behaviors does the firm want to see in its partners, managers, and staff?
- *Assessing future leaders' fit with needed competencies and skills.* How well does each of the people with high potential for leadership measure up to the determined competencies required for their current and future positions?
- *Developing plans to close any skill or competency gaps.* What will the firm do to help these high potential individuals continue to grow into the type of professional the firm wants to see in the future?

On the other end of the spectrum, the partner group should be addressing the following issues:

- The firm's overall strategy and direction
- Business models and modes of operation
- Governance processes necessary to run the business
- Equity reallocation, so the right people have a say in running the business
- Compensation framework that supports the firm's strategy and change initiatives

It is necessary to address these issues to make the changes that create long-term sustainability and viability of the firm. Crisis planning and orderly succession planning strategies are tools that firms should be using to protect their organizations' value and future.

Component Parts of an Orderly Succession Plan

At the end of the day, orderly succession is about creating

- a system driven by strategy,
- an organization that supports constant change, and
- an operating model created around the idea of interchangeable parts (people fill roles with expected competencies) rather than building roles and competencies around specific individuals.

With this in mind, each chapter of this book focuses on a major component section we recommend your succession plan address in order to build a quality and robust plan promoting near-seamless transition from one generation of leaders to the next. Volume 1 will focus on the general and conceptual issues to be addressed in the plan, while the corresponding field guide will provide whoever is in charge of implementing this plan with more of an in-depth approach as well as tools and resources to utilize.

Chapter 2—Start With Strategy

The first step is to develop your firm's strategic plan. We have included it as the first step because many firms don't do this. If you already have a plan, you have operationalized it, and it drives change to your partner and management compensation priorities, then you are good to go and can probably skip this chapter. If you haven't implemented a plan yet (meaning that you might have a plan, but it is not fully operationalized and it does not change compensation), then chapter 2 will give you some insight about how that process should work and what should come out of it. As well, volume 2, chapter 2 will give you a step-by-step approach to implementing planning in your firm.

Chapter 3—Clean Up Your Operations

Once you have a strategic plan with tactics, action items, timelines, and assignments, it is time to move to the next step in the succession management process: cleaning up operations. This step is about running your firm in a way so that it provides the greatest benefits and value to you. Because benefits and value are in the eye of the beholder, and are often framed by strategy, once you get to this step, it is time to make those changes you have known for years you should be making. This typically comes down to issues such as the following:

- Raising your rates to be in line with the market
- Either rehabilitating or running off marginal clients
- Developing or dismissing marginal employees

- Investing in the current technology that will support your business and your strategy
- Making sure that you are acting in a way that is both efficient and effective (such as passing work down wherever possible to create more leverage)
- Holding clients accountable to delivering their work per the engagement agreement or requesting more money to do the work through a change order process
- Ensuring that all of your people are returning a profit to the firm, and more.

Don't do what so many firms do and wait until right before the senior partners retire (doing so in order to get maximum value for the firm) to put your house in order . Put it in order now and reap the years of benefits and value that this effort will produce.

Chapter 4—Identify and Describe Your Business Model

Your choice of business model, with the two most common being the Eat What You Kill (EWYK) and the One-Firm, or what we call the Building a Village (BAV) concept, will drive many of the choices you will have to make to create and effectively implement your succession plan. For example, if you are an EWYK firm, when it comes time for a partner to retire and sell his or her interest in the firm, that partner needs to see if anyone wants to buy his or her clients, with the partners of the firm having a first right of refusal. In an EWYK model of operations, the common buyout is based on client book, paid based on client retention, and paid out over four to five years without interest. Under this model, you get to enjoy the spoils of your success while working (in other words, you milk the cash cow). When it is time to leave, you sell your relationships for what you can get and hope whoever buys your book of business will keep most of your clients. Because the purchase is based on retention, the buyer's motivation and integrity is critical to you getting paid because the buyer could just cherry-pick a few clients, pay $1.00 or even $1.50 for each dollar of revenue, and still leave the retiring partner with little to show for his or her hard work over the years. Under this model, everything is a negotiation, from what clients are sold, to what the retiring partner might be allowed to do work-wise going forward, to any other term that either side is interested in discussing. This is because under the EWYK model, the succession plan is simply to sell your book of business and hope you have someone who is both willing to buy it at a reasonable price and willing to work hard to maintain those client relationships. In this model, the retiring partner doesn't have a real interest in the firm to sell because the partners do what they want, how they want, when they want, at the price they want, follow whatever rules they want, and have built a silo organization within the larger firm. Therefore, it makes sense that the firm should not be obligated to buy out the retiring partner at a formula fixed price when the firm had little to no say over what the partner was building in the first place.

Succession planning under the BAV model is quite different from planning under the EWYK model. There are a number of ways to value the firm in this situation, and one big advantage of using this model is that it is fair for the partner to expect some specificity regarding the terms of the buyout when they are bought out at the time of retirement. Because the remaining partners are obligated to buy out the retiring partner (based on whatever valuation method they choose—we discuss all of this in greater detail in chapter 5), that obligation comes with a number of expectations or conditions. Those conditions are that the firm will be ready to

- build and cement relationships with the retiring partner's clients in order to retain them;
- replace the retiring partner with sufficient physical capacity to get the work done;
- replace the retiring partner's technical skills so that someone can actually do the work that the retiring partner was doing.

After you have developed your strategy, the second step in the plan is to align that strategy with a business model that will support the changes you want to make and implement. Once you choose your business model and agree to be held accountable to operating under it, it is time to move to the next step in the succession management process.

Chapter 5—Examine Retirement Benefits

We cover this issue early because, for many organizations, change requires the most senior partners to give up some of their control, including how the resources of the firm will be reallocated. Our experience is that if you don't resolve this issue early, you will never get any traction for change. It is one thing to ask senior partners to make changes when they know what value they are trying to protect as well as the risks they are undertaking to protect that value. It is an entirely different story when you are asking that same group to take risks without any assurance about their reward for allowing the changes to occur.

So, we need to start this chapter by determining the valuation method for retirement. This will include the following:

- What is being sold
- At what price
- On which date
- Under what installment terms
- At what interest rate
- The value of the ownership interest
- The value of the capital
- Under what terms and conditions and penalties, and so on

After you have determined the preceding items, vesting requirements need to be outlined in order for the retirement benefit to be fully determinable. Sections addressing the following points need to be laid out in detail to close the loop on the retirement issue:

- Vesting
- Penalties for leaving with adequate notice
- Penalties for early retirement with notice
- Mandatory sale of ownership

Between the high level review of these issues in this book, and a detailed coverage of them in volume 2, you will have plenty of best practice ideas to consider as you make your way down the path to clear retirement benefit strategy.

Chapter 6—Describe Governance, Roles, and Responsibilities

We will take a detailed dive into this area. It is the most critical part to get right, or close to right, yet is often the area with the greatest need for some maintenance and repair. This chapter is about roles and responsibilities, powers and limitations, and being clear about who can do what and where the lines of authority are drawn. This is a foundational step if you want to have any real chance of implementing accountability throughout your organization. We will cover the roles and responsibilities of

- the board or partner group,
- various board committees,
- the managing partner, and
- various roles of line partners, from client service partner to practice leader, technical partner, and more.

Chapter 7—Establish Voting Rights, Decision Making, and Equity Distribution or Redistribution

In this section of the succession plan, we will cover the importance of moving away from the most common general consensus model for making decisions to one based on voting and voting thresholds. This, as another part of governance, is critical to supporting accountability, as well.

In addition to the voting process, equity distribution and redistribution are key. As partners retire, new partners are admitted, and partnership shifts around, it is essential that the mechanism to manage the distribution and redistribution of equity is strong and fully functioning. We will take you through a case study to demonstrate how this often gets out of hand and why taking your eye off of this area can set your firm up so that succession management is dead from the start.

Chapter 8—Define the Managing Partner Role

The purpose of this provision is to make sure that it is clear how the managing partner is elected, for what term, and most importantly, how he or she is protected if removed from that role. The job differs depending on whether it is being filled under the EWYK or BAV models. As an example, in order to do the job properly under the BAV model, the managing partner needs to be in a position to consider the firm as his or her largest and most important client. This usually requires a reduction in managed book size, so that the firm can become the managing partner's key priority together with an expected compensation package for filling that role. Therefore, when a partner is removed from the role of managing partner, he or she needs to be assured that the firm is committed to putting him or her back into a line-partner position that is consistent with where he or she would have been had he or she not taken the managing partner position.

Chapter 9—Build Capacity for Long-Term Sustainability

Next, the firm should outline the strategy for continually building the necessary capacity to replace the retiring partner and create more leverage for the remaining partners to make the financial aspects of your operational model work. This area of the succession plan has multiple components:

- Developing real people management skills
- Learning how to develop people more quickly
- Closing competency gaps

Chapter 10—Transition Client and Referral Relationships

This chapter reviews how the firm is going to hold partners accountable for transitioning their clients and how they will be paid during that slow-down period. This process actually has quite a bit of trickle-down effect to it because typically, once a transition plan is created for a retiring partner, a similar plan has to be generated for multiple positions below the departing partner in order for each level to free up capacity to take on the work being handed down.

Chapter 11—Describe the Admission to Ownership and Development Process

We are big fans of bringing in partners at accrual basis book value buy-in and then buying them out when their sweat equity has earned them retirement benefits. This, in turn, requires vesting, which usually doesn't even result in even partial retirement benefits being earned until around age 60. Way too many firms have partners buy in at market. The problem with that model is that if someone buys in at market, the firm has no good argument as to why someone can't leave any time he or she wishes and be bought out at market (that is, why would I pay market and get anything less than market when I decide to leave?).

A major reason organizations bring in younger partners is to create a succession strategy. They need people who will be ready to take over and run the firm when it is time for the senior partners to go. Therefore, we don't want partners leaving anytime they want to go, but in an orderly fashion once they have worked for the firm long enough as a partner and reached retirement age.

Chapter 12—Build a Strong Partner Group

Logically, if we are going to talk about people buying in, we also need to talk about people leaving. Because we discussed departure for retirement earlier, we now need to address other departures, including voluntary or involuntary withdrawal from the firm. When you outline this section in your agreements, you need to address a number of areas associated with people leaving your firm and competing with it:

- Benefits available when leaving and competing or not competing with the firm
- Penalties for leaving and taking staff or clients
- Vote required to terminate a partner

Your firm should not be in the business of creating spin-off competitors, so you need to think through how you will address partners who leave and take clients or staff to compete with your firm. The voting percentage required to terminate a partner is also critical to succession management. As a firm grows, it becomes more and more critical to hold partners accountable to following systems, processes, and procedures. When a partner will not comply, you need to first be able to motivate him or her to comply by penalizing him or her financially. If that doesn't work, you need to be able to penalize him or her even more financially. And if that doesn't motivate the partner to change, then you need to be able to let them go. One of the biggest weaknesses we see is firms adopting such a high voting threshold to fire someone that it is almost impossible to let someone go. For the sake of the firm's long-term viability, you have to have a way to cut partners from the herd who have made it clear that they will not comply with operational policy.

Chapter 13—Establish Processes and Procedures for Retired Partners Still Working for the Firm

Next, you need to establish rules of conduct and operational processes for those ex-partners who retire and still want to continue working in some capacity for the firm. From our perspective, this means they will be working differently than they did before. Even more importantly, they won't be working for the firm at all if the firm doesn't specifically invite them to continue working (and we believe the maximum length of that invitation should be one year at a time).

Chapter 14—Define the Maximum Payout Process and Other Buyout-Related Issues

To ensure that the firm can pay those who have retired or left without putting the firm's sustainability in jeopardy, a policy must be developed to put a cap on the maximum amount of money that can be paid out to departed partners. You need a section of the succession plan that addresses the maximum amount of payout in any year. Chapter 14 walks readers through this process.

Chapter 15—Create a Partner Accountability and Compensation Plan

This is the section of the succession plan that creates the most angst because it is often much more nebulous than the current compensation formulas in place, is built on trusting the system, and is defined as constantly changing from the outset. The framework needs to be flexible enough to dramatically change every time the firm's strategies or priorities change. The job of the partner compensation system is to motivate partners to achieve their part of the firm's strategic plan. Compensation is an incredibly effective tool an organization can use to reward those people who are contributing to the firm's success and make it clear to those who are not that they need to change their behaviors. The partner compensation framework needs to be supported by firm policy in such a way that it enables the managing partner to hold the partners accountable for achieving whatever goals are assigned to them. At the same time, it has to be set up with enough balance that the managing partner doesn't gain so much control through the compensation process that he or she is in a position to usurp powers that are reserved for the board.

Chapter 16—Address Death and Disability in Your Buy-Sell and Retirement Policies

Finally, your succession plan has to address how death and partial or full disability are handled when they occur. We suggest that provisions addressing buyouts for death and disability take into account that someone's departure under these conditions can place the firm at some serious financial risk, if only due to the inability to properly transition client and referral relationships and develop the capacity for someone to take over for the departed partner. As well, special attention needs to be paid to situations when a partner is in and out of disability over time and how that will be addressed by the firm. These critical areas need to be addressed in a way that is fair and equitable to both the departing partner and the firm, and they normally are covered separately under death, partial disability, and total disability provisions.

In Conclusion

Our stance, in everything we do working with firms, in what we write in our books and what we talk about when we speak, is that succession is the natural and seamless evolution of managing a well-run firm. But if your firm is not following best practices, then succession will turn a spotlight on the firm's every weakness. We believe that if you take the time to think through and address each of the topics in this book, you will be more than ready for succession. As well, you will be one of the few firms on the planet with a truly robust succession plan to form, guide, and direct your upcoming change in leadership.

Good succession management is about ensuring that when key people leave, the firm doesn't redefine everything it is doing but continues to operate on sound foundational principles, with the only real difference being a change in *who* is filling key leadership roles and responsibilities.

Depending on your firm and your people, it can take a minimum of three to five years to develop someone or for people to take over. Succession is rarely about just one position—it is usually about playing an organization-wide game of Musical Chairs. For every person you move up, someone has to fill the void created by a promotion. That is why creating a viable succession process can take more than five years: because succession affects the firm at every level. Although one person might be ready to step into a key role in the firm, if that same person has not developed a replacement for his or her current position, the promotion solves one problem and potentially creates another.

The concept of succession planning may sound simple, but it takes time to work through all the moving parts and put together a plan to manage them. The longer you delay, the more likely you will be ready to make only the first move of a multi-move play. This will not end well and will likely result in having fewer options to consider. Life is about options—creating options and making choices among those options. The fewer options you create, the more you might find yourself trapped by the choices that remain.

Our profession is undergoing a great deal of change right now, and we believe it will undergo significantly more change as the baby boom generation retires in force. We believe that many CPAs will soon find themselves putting their single biggest asset, their business, at high risk if they don't start planning now to compensate for these changes. This text and its companion, *Securing the Future, Volume 2: Implementing Your Firm's Succession Plan*, were created to help you create a viable plan for your firm.

We hope you enjoy the journey and the process!

Chapter 2: Start With Strategy

Strategy Should Drive the Rest of Your Decisions

If you don't already have one, your firm needs a shared commitment to a strategic plan or an overall strategic direction. Why? Because planning is an essential ingredient to success. Theodore Roosevelt said it well: When you aim at nothing, you'll hit it every time. Even if you have an updated, compelling plan for the future shared by all the firm's partners, are you communicating it to everyone else? Think of it this way:

> Picture 50 ants carrying a small twig with the objective of maneuvering in a northerly direction. What happens when 40 ants push north and the other 10 are attempting to march west?

The answer, of course, is chaos. The ants moving west cause two problems. First, they slow the progress of the overall group. Second, within a short period of time, the entire group will find themselves far off course. They might even find that their movement has been circular.

This same scenario with ants going in different directions happens all the time in CPA firms when some people are not aligned with the overall strategy. The firm ends up with chaos and spin. Often, CPAs will say, "You know, we decided that we were going to do something during our strategy session, but we came back and ended up doing something different." That's probably because you didn't get everybody pushing in the same direction—you either didn't have a truly shared strategic direction or vision, or you didn't make it clear that whatever is decided in group as a firm will be what everyone is held accountable to accomplishing.

In order for a firm to continuously improve performance, everyone needs to have a clear sense of purpose (mission) and direction (vision). The principle is simple:

> The more people you have consciously working toward a common goal, the greater the likelihood of its achievement.

By formalizing the planning process, you can better inform the people, with partners being among the many key people to keep informed. Because the planning process defines the firm's strategic targets and identifies the actions required to reach them, everyone has a better understanding of their roles. This understanding synchronizes individual efforts, thus promoting departmental or group achievement, culminating in the accomplishment of overall firm or corporate objectives.

We realize that many of you might feel that this planning stuff is soft, overrated, and only marginally useful. However, our experience is that most businesses fail due to the lack of good basic business practices. Yes, your firm may have become pretty successful without having gone through this type of planning, but how much more successful might it have been with it, and how much better prepared for succession and the future might it be once the planning is done?

Lack of planning is the root cause of many to most problems and a strong contributor to mediocrity of organizational performance, so making sure that your organization consistently spends quality time planning may be the most important role you have to play as a business owner. Here are a couple of additional ways to think about this:

- Without an agreed-upon plan, every idea is an equally viable opportunity. Planning is the tool that helps you perform a sanity check about which ideas make the most sense to pursue based on the current direction you have chosen.

- Without an agreed-upon strategy, the firm doesn't have a way to easily manage the efforts of the partners. A firm plan allows a sanity check against the personal initiatives the various partners want to perform. Without an agreed-upon plan, stifling the direction of one partner by management simply appears to be bullying or dominating behavior. With a plan, management is in the preferred position of being able to hold up a mirror to a partner, asking him or her to defend how their efforts are supporting the firm's direction. Without a plan, accountability seems like personal preference. With a plan, accountability seems like an appropriate management response.

Thinking Strategically

Your planning process might start with some external trend analysis to identify what's likely to change over the next few years. This trend analysis would involve looking at potential changes with respect to your target markets and ideal client profiles as well as your targeted service offerings. You'll want to think about changes in conditions that might result in changes in your clients' needs over the long term and how you can be a part of meeting those needs as they change. You also should consider the nature of competition you now face and how that may change over time.

You'll also want to do some introspection:

- What, objectively, can you cite as key internal weaknesses that you should address based on trends you see in your business?

- How about key competitive strengths? Nearly everyone with whom we've talked lays claim to great client service and depth and breadth of technical expertise as key strengths. We suspect that's possible, but can every firm have the same top two strengths? (Just some food for thought.)

- What about your own personal three-year vision? What would you like to see and be doing in three years, and how does the firm fit into this personal vision?

Planning is dynamic. Today's plans affect tomorrow's reality, tomorrow's reality influences tomorrow's plans, tomorrow's plans affect the future's reality, and so on. In a perfect world, planning and reality could pictorially be demonstrated as two straight

Figure 2-1

When there is an absence of planning, any real chance of forward movement is often stifled.

lines overlapping each other. In a controlled world, plans could remain constant because we eventually would fine-tune reality to match the plan. But in our world, which is, more often than not, out of control, both plans and reality are moving targets. So, our expectations need to be put into perspective.

First, don't expect reality to emulate the plan. The best we can hope for is that the two begin to parallel each other at some point in the future. The net of this is that plans continually need to be monitored and adjusted so they are consistent with the resources available. Firm performance needs to be continually monitored and adjusted so the end results approximate the plan.

In the absence of planning and plan monitoring, your company is likely to zig and zag too often and for too long, as in figure 2-1. This, in turn, can stifle any significant forward movement. Scarce resources, such as cash, capability, and capacity, are often wasted on efforts that do not contribute to the organization's long-term survival and profitability.

The question of success often boils down to whether the partner group can become and remain focused on shared strategic goals. Every time a firm veers off course, it can take months or even years to reverse the momentum. The more entrepreneurial the partners, the more "opportunities" they see in the marketplace, and the more likely these opportunities will distract them. By planning, and planning often, you can avoid decisions that spread your firm into conflicting directions. Thus, you can minimize the mistake and recovery cycle or the zig-zag effect, thereby making a significant contribution to your bottom line. As mentioned previously, without a good idea about your strategic direction or vision for the future, everything looks like an opportunity to pursue, regardless of whether it actually is. In fact, strategy is as much about what you're *not* going to do as it is about what you hope to accomplish.

Strategic Planning Overview

Strategic planning consists of a long-term view of the corporate strategy, direction, and objectives of your firm. The span of time covered will vary based on each company's unique situation and industry. In today's world of fast-paced change, many small to medium-sized businesses we know are looking at three to four years as a maximum planning horizon, especially for professional service firms, technology businesses, and other organizations that undergo rapid change.

Strategic planning is the mental positioning of a company at some specific point in the future. By helping your organization formalize this mental position, you can begin to build the bridge that will link today with the future.

Getting Started

So, where do you start when you are either creating or revising a strategic plan? As we mentioned previously, you might want to start with some external and internal trend analyses and then craft your individual vision for the future. Next, you'll want to review or create a mission statement, a core values statement, and a three- to four-year organization vision statement. In their work *Built to Last*, authors James Collins and Jerry Porras reviewed the results of research they had performed on pairs of publicly traded companies.[1] Each of the companies in a pair was from the same industry. One had been successful over the years. The other had been wildly successful. The research attempted to find causes for the difference between being really great and just being good. As it turned out, the really successful companies were those who had a strong core philosophy to keep them grounded in what is really important to them, coupled with an energizing vision of the future to pull them into the future and keep the company in a process of reinvention to stay relevant to customers or clients. Let's look at each of these concepts in a little more detail in the following sections.

Core Philosophy

The core philosophy of a firm normally is a combination of its core values and its core purpose or mission statement. *Core values* are the guiding principles that the company uses to conduct its day-to-day business, both internally and externally. Typically, there are a handful of key principles or business values that set a company apart and identify who it is. They answer questions such as *what do we believe in here?* and *how do we conduct ourselves?* For example, one of our core values at Succession Institute is "actively pursue lifelong learning," while another is "we don't pander to management to protect our fees." The core values need to be applicable to your own organization and they need to be *values in action*. It's one thing to tout "mutual respect" as a core value, but another to scold your employees publicly in the hallway, for example. Another example comes to mind from our meeting with the senior management team of a large company, during which they listed "work-life balance" as a core value. When we asked them what part of consistently working 60- to 65-hour weeks reflected that value, they then agreed that "work-life balance" was perhaps more appropriately reflected as an element of their vision for the future. This concept probably applies to many other CPA firms, as well.

The core purpose, or the mission, explains what the company does. It answers the questions *why does the company exist?* and *what is its focus?* Notice that these questions are focused on the client or customer because the corporate mission, in order to achieve the maximum effectiveness,should be client or customer driven. The issues are not *where are we?* but rather, *what do we do that adds value to our clients?* Our mission, for instance, is "to facilitate our clients' long-term success." It doesn't say exactly how we do that because that's covered in our overall strategy and definition of markets, offerings, and so on.

Long-Term Vision

An energizing vision describes where the company is headed—what it will be doing and for whom at the end of the planning horizon (for example, in three or four years). It describes the ideal future you want to create for your organization. It should describe

---

[1] James C. Collins and Jerry I. Porras, *Built to Last* (New York: HarperCollins, 1994).

this future in terms of customer or client offerings as well as in terms relative to your workforce—what it's like to work at your organization. It answers the questions *just how good could it be in the future?* as well as *who will be my clients in three years?* and *what will my clients need from me then?*

This leads us to the next point regarding your vision. The market(s) you serve now may not be the market(s) you serve in the future. This is an important issue to get some shared agreement on and commitment to among your partner group. Strategic planning addresses these questions. One of the main objectives behind defining the firm vision is to think through where your market will be in the future. By performing this exercise, you can help your firm devise a plan that will allow it to deliver services that are in demand in this future market.

Consider MTV as an example. Assume for a moment that MTV segmented the "music video-watching market" into age groups (one of many probable demographics). Let's further assume, for the sake of discussion, that MTV's customer profile is kids aged 12–19. How successful would MTV be today had they chosen a strategic direction purely by answering the questions *where am I?* and *where am I going?* We maintain they would be out of business. When you consider the questions *who are my customers?* and *where are they going?* opportunities and obstacles more clearly come to mind. If the true customers are now 12–19 years old, then next year they will be 13–20 years old, and the year after 14–21 years old, and so on. However, if the customers are an age group, then each year, anyone aged 12–19 would fit the profile.

So, for example, if MTV did decide that its product served the original 12–19 age group, then MTV would be playing the music now aired by VH1, and in 2030, the music would likely be classified as "golden oldies." If MTV decided its market was the age group 12–19, then every year, they would have to research the music tastes of those from 8–11 years of age in order to begin preparing for the format shifts required to maintain their market share. On one hand, this distinction seems so obvious it is almost embarrassing to mention. On the other hand, it is the kind of subtlety that organizations miss every day that eventually puts them at a disadvantage, if not into bankruptcy.

Figure 2-2

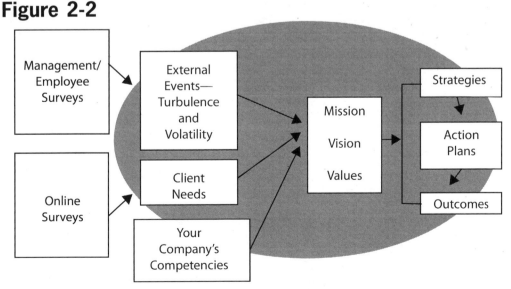

The Overall Planning Process

Strategies, Action Plans, and Metrics

To put these concepts in perspective, consider the following:

Core purpose	WHAT you do
Core values	HOW you conduct yourselves in doing it
Vision	WHERE you are headed collectively

As soon as the mission, vision, and values are identified and complete, the emphasis shifts toward the identification of the steps that will facilitate the achievement of the vision. As you conducted your external and internal analysis and review, you likely identified internal strengths and weaknesses as well as external challenges and opportunities. As a result of all the work you've done, you'll see that a handful of key initiatives or strategies will need to be addressed to leverage strengths, work on critical weaknesses, and take advantage of strategic opportunities, while avoiding or minimizing the potential damage of challenges as you move toward your vision. Once you've identified key areas that require attention and established goals around them, then you lay out plans to accomplish those goals. Once an idea becomes measurable, monitorable, assignable, and accountable, you are done; it's time to move on to the next topic of interest.

As you're creating action plans, together with performance metrics to monitor success, you also need to budget for the changes in your operations resulting from implementing the action plans. Of course, when it comes to establishing budgets, this is one task CPAs can do in their sleep. Finally, no budget should be considered complete until incentives are developed and put in place that will reward those who achieve or exceed expectations. Without incentives, there's no clear thread connecting the beginning of this process to its end. People do what they get paid to do. If you come back from a planning retreat and everyone continues to be paid solely on their book of business, production, realization, and so on, then that's what they'll focus on, rather than implementation of the organizational changes needed to achieve the new vision.

We see this time and time again. A firm's partners get together and they lay out a nice business plan that says, "Here's our strategy," and that's the last time they look at it. Even if they do go to the extra effort of looking at it from time to time, there are no incentives tied to it, and that's where they tend to drop the ball. You need an incentive pay plan that reinforces the statement "If these are our goals, we will stop doing certain activities and start doing these other activities that support the strategic vision and goals." Without a focus on new behaviors, some of which will take time to implement and bear fruit, everything becomes too short-term focused—that is, what we did this last hour, day, or week, rather than what we are doing to put ourselves in a better position a year or two years from now. The next thing you know, it is two years later and your partner group is asking, "How did we end up here?"

The interesting part, or often, the sad part, of it is that sometimes firms get caught on the proverbial hamster wheel, with each year getting a little worse, requiring them to run a little harder and faster just to stay even. This run on the hamster wheel will continue until the firm is willing to start making an investment in the long term. It is about efficiency versus effectiveness. *Efficient* is doing the work yourself because the client wants it now, and no one else has the skills to do it. *Effective* is about recognizing that if you don't develop someone to do this, you will always be the one who has to stay late to get it done. Firms choose efficiency over effectiveness regularly. Planning helps organizations choose both—how to operate efficiently *without* sacrificing long-term effectiveness.

By implementing an incentive program, you begin to create an environment that holds people accountable for doing what it takes for the long-term success and effectiveness of the firm.

Accountability leads to accomplishment.

Creating a system in which people are held responsible for their work is such a simple principle, yet few firms implement it; or, if they do, they don't implement it correctly. The widespread lack of accountability and disincentives we see in practices throughout North America only reemphasizes the real need to pay more attention to this area. We discuss compensation systems further in chapter 15, so don't worry, we have far more to share on the topic of managing accountability and performance.

Some Typical Strategic Initiatives

You might be wondering what types of common strategic initiatives a CPA firm might need to pursue to achieve its long-term vision. The answer here depends on your particular firm and all the facts and circumstances surrounding the firm's desired vision, so no one size fits all here. However, we can tell you that it's fairly common to see some version of the following at many firms:

- Partner accountability and compensation
- Attracting, retaining, and developing people
- Growth, business development, and client retention
- Infrastructure consistency and efficiency
- Improved communication and transparency

Partner Accountability and Compensation

If you've attempted to implement previous strategic initiatives before and realized less-than-pleasing results, you probably are suffering from what we term "Poor Account-ability Syndrome." One of the first areas that need to be addressed to implement a robust succession plan is that of holding partners accountable. This can be very difficult and controversial with some partners, especially after they've become accustomed to not being accountable for much of anything over time. There are ways to deal with this, and we cover them in more detail in chapter 15. It should be no surprise, however, that compensation incentives or disincentives are a critical part of the solution.

Attracting, Retaining, and Developing People

This is perhaps the number one problem today in CPA firms of all sizes, and it likely will continue to be so. Although some firms are actively addressing finding, retaining, and developing people, too few are doing a really good job of it. Furthermore, with our profession's unemployment rate at roughly 3 percent nationally, if you don't walk the talk about taking care of and developing your people, they have plenty of options with other organizations courting them to move. Our personal experience shows that once a firm decides an employee is not pulling his or her weight, it takes an average of two more years to let them go. Think about the message this sends to our good employees and how it furthers the very real perception that they are carrying the water for our bad employees. There is much more to cover on this topic, which you will find in chapter 9.

Growth, Business Development, and Client Retention

These are often tricky issues for firms. In some firms, just about everyone at the partner and manager levels are tapped out as far as productive capacity. They can't do any more work. So, while this issue usually is among the top strategic planning issues, doing more business development seems counterintuitive because they don't have anyone who can do the work, unless the partners just decide to work more hours. The partners talk about developing their people so they can hand more work down, but they don't—and won't—make any time to train them, so more business just turns into more work for the partners. All of this, then, comes back to governance: holding partners accountable for doing what they are supposed to do and not allowing them to act like managers. When they live up to their partner role, then they will make time to get out in front of their top clients, creating greater client loyalty to the firm due to this proactive approach while also finding more work and attracting more referrals.

Infrastructure, Consistency, and Efficiency

Although your firm can bring in all the work your partners sell, unless you're turning a respectable profit on that work, it can become an exercise in futility. As competition continues for work and people, driving up the costs of people while driving down the revenue from the work, firms must pay greater attention to their consistency in doing the work as well as their efficiency in getting that work done. For example, although it is common to find audit work being done the same way regardless of who is leading a project, the same is rarely true for tax. In many firms, staff members have to change how they approach the work depending on who the partner in charge of that work is. To make matters worse, rather than work going to the next available resource, many firms queue up work to go to specific people, making the entire process even more inefficient. Unless firms make serious progress toward becoming more consistent and efficient, they can easily end up being the highly priced, high cost provider of many commodity compliance services, which we would say is a "going out of business" strategy. The lean processes originally introduced into the world of manufacturing have been picked up by other industries, including construction and personal services as well as public accounting firms. What are you doing to create leaner processes in your firm?

Improved Communication and Transparency

We rarely find an organization in which improved communication and transparency isn't one of the key strategic objectives. And it makes perfect sense that it is. How can we expect everyone to work together toward a common strategy and goals if we don't take the time to share those goals? How can we hold anyone accountable if we haven't made clear what is expected? How can we develop people without an understanding of the importance of this process to the firm's future success? How can we change consistency and efficiency without highlighting how our current processes are hurting the firm while costing it dearly? Without better communications and greater transparency, how can the firm build the kind of trust internally that will motivate its people to change while providing those same people the comfort of knowing that through change the firm can get better, faster, and stronger?

It doesn't help that many in our profession are wired such that the same traits that make them terrific technical problem solvers also tend to make them men and women of few words. So extra effort and attention is needed in this area—but the focus will pay off for you.

In Conclusion

In your firm, you'll likely see one or more of these initiatives crop up as areas needing attention when you conduct your strategic planning. Logically, you will have an additional initiative or two that are specific to your firm, as well. But you will find that many initiatives are integrated with others, and to be truly effective, firms often need to holistically address multiple initiatives simultaneously. For example, partners need to manage growth through business development and client retention (because that is one of their primary job duties), but that effort also has to be coupled with developing talent, improving systems, engraining accountability, and improving communication and transparency throughout the firm, or the development initiative will fail due to an inability to perform.

The same is true with so many initiatives CPA firms are trying to address—they are interrelated. Through strategy, firms can prioritize and tie these initiatives together to ensure the integrated parts are working to support each other and forward the firm's progress.

The key here is to not overextend yourself. Limit the initiatives to a handful and use a focused, rifle approach, rather than a shotgun approach, to direct your scarce resources. Stay on top of implementation and outcomes. Diligence here will pay off with a high return on investment in your strategic initiatives.

Get your strategy process underway while considering the ideas found in this book, and get ready to see some significant changes in your operations, your profits, and your overall success.

Chapter 3: Clean Up Your Operations

Get the Basics Right

To position your firm for succession or any major change, the first thing you need to do is clean up the operations. Firms mostly move at the speed of inertia, which is a simple way of saying they just keep doing what they have always done, with an occasional effort to do what they have always done a little faster.

Cleaning up your operations means far more than just creating a positive bottom line after market-based owner compensation. It means that you have systems, processes, and policies in place to allow the firm to function effectively and efficiently regardless of who is in the driver's seat.

It also means that you create a culture of operating that is formalized so that everyone knows what is expected, what is outside of their authority, and what is within their powers. This culture should be created with such clarity that everyone is empowered to be a watchdog protecting the core values of the organization. This is the kind of organization that can stand the test of time and leadership change because new bad management practices, which will constantly emerge, are attacked by the firm's personnel like antibiotics assaulting a bacteria—the bacteria is neutralized before any real damage is done.

In this chapter, we will address some fundamental issues you should consider handling regardless of the business model or exit strategy that you choose. As you read through this material and the corresponding chapter in *Securing the Future, Volume 2: Implementing Your Firm's Succession Plan*, you'll see a list of key performance metrics that can help owners better manage their firms. We recognize that some firms monitor substantially more performance measures than we've listed, and that's fine. The metrics here represent a starting point for some good discussion and perhaps an opportunity to take a fresh look at how you're running your business.

Information Systems and Performance Metrics

Although this may seem obvious to everyone, you need to have a database of practice statistics to help you monitor your relative success. For those buying, selling, or merging (regardless of direction up or down), those same statistics will help you prove your case for the value or pooling interest you feel you deserve. Although a surprising number of owners regularly review their firm statistics, and many even compare them to best practice benchmarks, the exercise is often one of justification or rationalization rather than trying to determine how to improve the firm. Because these owners don't pay much attention or give much weight to these statistics to guide their process improvement efforts, they are likely

- to utilize sloppy reporting systems for pulling this information together,
- to receive the data often after it's too late and too old to be most useful, and
- not to track the operating metrics as comprehensively as they should be.

We are no different than our clients, although we always make exceptions for ourselves. We should be running our firms more by the numbers (which should be tied to our strategy), just as we advise our clients to do.

Performance Metrics

So, what are some of the metrics you should be monitoring regularly to help you better manage your firm and position it for succession? The following are a few key metrics that can help you. The good news is that these same statistics are valuable to anyone who is interested in getting a thumbnail sketch of what's going on at your practice. There are many more metrics that you can track, but for our current purposes, we'd like to start with those presented below in table 3-1:

Table 3-1

Total Hours Worked	Total of chargeable and nonchargeable time by person, staff level, department, or other insightful grouping of staff and partners.
Total Chargeable Hours	Chargeable hours by person, staff level, department, or other insightful grouping of staff and partners.
Total Nonchargeable Hours	Nonchargeable hours by person, staff level, department, or other insightful grouping of staff and partners.
Gross Production	Amount of total charges generated in the firm (chargeable hours × hourly billing rates) by person, staff level, department, or other insightful grouping.
Net Revenues	This is your "billings." Amount actually billed after adjustments for write-ups and write-downs by person, staff level, department, or other insightful grouping of staff and partners.
Realization Percentage	This is net revenues / gross production. This should be by person, staff level, department, or other insightful grouping of staff and partners.

Full-Time Equivalents	This is the total number of full-time people in your firm: partners, directors, managers, seniors, staff and administration. Full-time people are easy—each person represents one full-time equivalent. For part-timers, you add their time together and make an evaluation. For example, two half-time personnel would be one full-time equivalent.
Net Revenues by Dept. or Service Grouping	Net revenues broken down by department or service grouping (Audit, Tax, Advisory, Wealth Management, and so on).
Net Revenues per Full-Time Equivalent (FTE)	This is the simple calculation of net revenues divided by FTE.
Net Revenues per Owner or Average Book Size	This is net revenues divided by the number of owners (often called Owner Book, or Owner Run).
Net Payroll / Revenues	This is payroll (excluding owners' pay) divided by net revenues. For some firms, depending on the ownership and compensation model, this might also include all guaranteed owners' salaries.
Leverage	Book managed by owner divided by *all* owners' personal billings on that book.
Net Book Revenues	Book managed by owner less all compensation paid to that owner.
Multiplier	Net revenues per person divided by their salary.
Growth in Net Revenues	This should be calculated both in absolute dollars and as a percentage of the prior period net revenues. In addition, budgets and plans should reference expected growth in net revenues.
Net Profits	Net profits are net revenues less all expenses excluding owner compensation. The only owner compensation that would typically be included as an expense would be for monies paid to nonequity owners.
Net Profit Percentage	Net profits as a percentage of net revenues.
Average Owner Compensation	Net profits divided by the number of owners.
Staff Turnover	For professional staff, the gross number of departures from the firm for any year.
Staff Additions	For professional staff, the gross number of new hires for the firm for any year.
Days of Revenues in Work-in-Process (WiP)	= WiP / (Net Revenues / 365)
Days of Revenues in Receivables	= Accounts Receivable / (Net Revenues / 365)
Marketing / Revenues	= Marketing costs (all marketing materials, sales materials, advertising programs, consultant time, and personnel solely supporting the marketing function) / Net Revenues
Technology / Revenues	= Technology costs (all expenditures for software, hardware, upgrades, repairs and maintenance, training conversion costs, and personnel solely supporting technology) / Net Revenues
Training (Continuing Professional Education) / Revenues	= CPE costs (all out-of-pocket costs associated with CPE for the firm and staff solely supporting the training function) / Net Revenues

Our System of Client Classification

We use an A-B-C-D scheme to classify clients, and we have included it as a tool here for you to review:

As a quick summary, "A" clients are the absolute top clients—they never squabble about fees, they appreciate your relationship with them, value you as a trusted adviser, and actively promote you to their friends and colleagues. "B" clients are "A" clients who can benefit from more of your services than you presently are providing, and, therefore, they are likely to be a little underserved. "C" clients are not bad clients; they just don't have much opportunity over and above the tax return or bookkeeping that you are now providing. "D" clients are those that should be an "A," "B," or "C" client, but you have some problems with them.

In every practice we've seen, from 10 percent to 30 percent of the clients provide 80 percent to 90 percent of the firm's volume and profit. These are your "A" and high "B" clients. By focusing more of your precious time on them, you can build even stronger relationships that benefit them and your firm. Get rid of the bad clients and you'll have time to devote to the other activities necessary for cleaning up your operations. In fact, the first step in cleaning up operations should be to evaluate, rank, and upgrade your clients, leading to increased capacity within your firm. This is something every firm should do, whether the owners are thinking about walking away and turning out the lights, selling, or merging in either direction. In the worst case, you can work a little less and make the same or even more money than you have been earning. In the best case, you open up significant upside potential for the long run. Think of it this way. Let's say you have a $400,000 practice. Let's say you raise your fees in the following manner with these consequences:

"A" clients =$100,000. You raise your fees 10 percent; this runs off 10 percent of your clients, with nets fees from this group next year being $99,000.

"B" clients = $100,000. You raise your fees 10%; this runs off 10 percent of your clients, with net fees from this group next year being $99,000.

"C" clients = $100,000. You raise your fees 25 percent; this runs off 15 percent of your clients, with net fees from this group next year being $106,250.

"D" clients = $100,000. You raise your fees 75 percent with this group; this runs off 50 percent of your clients, with net fees from this group next year being $87,500.

The net result would be a reduction of about 25 percent of the time required to do the work, with a total reduction in fees of a little more than $8,000. Keep in mind that this scenario assumes the rate increase will run off some "A" and "B" clients, which is somewhat rare. Create your own math scenario. It just doesn't pay, either in time or money, to do work at discounted rates for marginal clients. Our personal experience is that you will not run off nearly as many clients as you think you will. As an offset, if you want to grow your practice, your freed-up time will allow you to find much better work than you lost; and as a side benefit for the future, the effort you just made raised the value of your firm.

You may be saying to yourself, "We already track that here," or "Why do we need to track that one?" with respect to each of the measures previously noted. While you can track, and probably should track, other performance measures, the preceding list will help you zero in on some low-hanging fruit for operational performance improvements. We have provided much more detail on calculations and implications of these metrics in volume 2.

Strategies for Improvement That Will Yield High Return on Investment

Now that you have a list of common performance metrics to help you identify areas where your firm could use a little more attention, we'd like to cover a few other areas where improvements can yield a high return on investment. In addition to monitoring your performance metrics and instituting appropriate changes to improve performance as needed, consider the following issues:

- Create capacity at the top
- Improve your overall profit stream
- Charge clients a fair fee
- Manage through the trough

Create Capacity at the Top

During the last few decades, public accounting firms have dramatically expanded the scope of services they offer. Many of these services have been in specialty areas, from being aligned by industries such as auto dealers or health care to specialized services such as business valuation or fraud detection. When these services are launched, they typically are championed by an owner, principal, or someone highly respected within the organization. Because some of these areas have sporadic demand or require a high level of expertise, firms often relied on these same senior people to manage the bulk of the work. In addition, as you will find out in chapter 4, in the EWYK model (or the Superstar model), the superstars take on all the work they can, and when they can't work anymore, they bring in people to help them so they can get more done in the same amount of time. This has driven a trend in small to midsized firms to build a workflow process that looks like an upside-down pyramid.

This operating environment, for many firms, functions something like what is shown in figure 3-1.

Figure 3-1

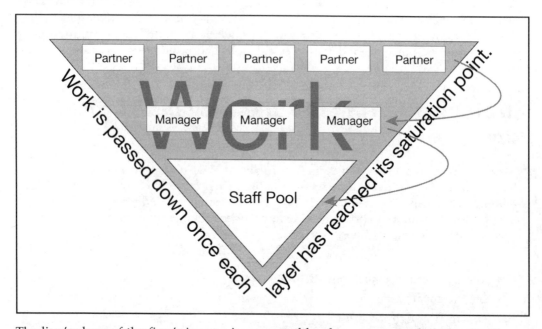

The lion's share of the firm's income is generated by the partners and managers. The partners and managers are very involved in the details of most client projects. The workflow hierarchy is a trickle-down approach. Partners do the technical work until they have worked all the hours they can stand, and the excess trickles down to the managers. The managers do the technical work until they have labored all they can stomach, and the remains trickle down to the staff pool. In each case, keeping the workers below busy is almost an afterthought.

It is as if these firms have an attitude that the subordinates are employed to do the work that their superiors don't want to do or are considered to be administrators providing assistance when needed. In the upside-down pyramid environment, partners and managers are overworked, and staff is underworked and poorly trained. There are a number of major problems created by this environment.

Partners Doing Non-Partner Work

Instead of pushing work down to the lowest level possible, work is performed by the most experienced person possible. The fees for much of the work we do as CPA firms are either fixed-in-fact or in-presumption. Obviously, fees are fixed-in-fact when a specific project price was specified. The fees are fixed-in-presumption when we do recurring work, like preparing a tax return each year, and the client assumes that this year's fees will be similar to those charged in previous years (unless the scope of the work changed). So, if you consider that much of a CPA's work is fixed in price, then using more experienced people than necessary to do the work could create larger write-downs or, even worse, consumes the most scarce resource a CPA firm has—the owner's time.

Some may take the position that more experienced people do the work faster so that write-downs are not a factor, but we would bet there is higher-level work the experienced people are avoiding that should be done by them instead. When partners or managers tie themselves up doing work that is below their capability, they are not only doing work someone else could do at a lower rate, but they are also diminishing the amount of time they can devote to higher value work that only they can do.

Undertrained Staff

Because upside-down pyramid firms follow a "work first, manage second" strategy, at every level of the firm, people are poorly trained. The common response to why is, "If I were to give this work to someone below me, I would have to spend so much time supervising them on the project that it is just quicker to do it myself."

Our response is that both the roles of partner and manager are based on the philosophy that you are supposed to get the work done through others. As a manager, that title is descriptive of your job—to manage. Otherwise, your title would be "doer." The next time you hear yourself utter the words, "It will take too much time to train my people to do this," then stop right there and remind yourself while it may take longer, your job is to train them so that they can do this work. Another classic reaction from this reversed workflow pyramid is that employees rarely get feedback on their work. Instead of the partner or manager sending back a list of errors for the originator to fix, the senior people reviewing the project just correct it and get it out the door.

Partner Conflict

There is little financial leverage in an upside-down pyramid, which creates economic frustration. Conflicts arise because of the disparity of roles and duties between partners. Some partners are stepping up and embracing their responsibilities, while others are functioning in the safe and unchallenging space of being glorified managers ("unchallenging" only because that is what they were doing before becoming a partner, so they are hiding in their previous jobs).

Hiring of Staff

The key resource—the potential source of competitive advantage for any service business—is its people and the intellectual capital they bring to bear on it. CPA firm owners need to ramp up their people management and development skills if they ever hope to retire and realize the full value of the firm they have built. Skilled talent is at a premium throughout the CPA profession and other industries, and it's not likely to get any better even in the next decade. As you know from surveys described in chapter 1, attracting talent and retaining talent typically show up as two of the top five issues. Everyone is looking to add skilled professionals, and no one is really finding them.

Many firms continue to pursue a strategy of attempting to hire experienced staff. However, in our opinion, regardless of how big you are or where you are located, when you find an experienced professional to fill an open position from outside the firm, you are either extremely lucky that someone's career and life needs happened to mesh with your firm's needs, or you are hiring someone else's problem and making them your problem. To be sure, there are some talented people who get hired into CPA firms through retained searches, but many of them are "hired guns" who will come to work for you at an outrageously high salary and then leave about 18 months later, either for a higher compensation package somewhere else or to leave before you realize they are never going to perform up to their hype or expectation.

So, what's the answer? You may not be pleased to read this, but building your own people right out of college has become about the only option that is truly reliable for the vast majority of firms we work with. It takes time, but this approach is a proven way to begin turning the upside-down pyramid right side up.

The good news is twofold. First, if you have several years until retirement, you can make this change and improve the value of the business for you and for those owners who are left in the firm after your departure. Second, because most firms are really bad at developing people, if you put effort and monitoring into this area, you likely will be able to build the typically experienced five-year person in only two to three years.

Improve Your Overall Profit Stream

Whether you are thinking about retiring, selling, merging, or just working in your firm for a long period of time without an exit strategy, if possible, you should take steps now to better secure your personal future as well as that of your firm. This urgency significantly rises in importance for those who wish to retire within the next few years. To be able to develop the most workable and beneficial retirement scenario, CPA firm owners need to be creating multiple options for their succession rather than just relying on one. All of those options are enhanced by improving your bottom line.

We've just mentioned the importance of creating capacity at the top and what that can do for you. Now, let's look at the overall profit stream and some ideas for enhancing it.

Too many professionals do not give adequate attention to overall profit stream. For many practice owners, the bottom line is "good enough," or they don't believe that there's much within their control to improve it. For some with specialized practices, there may not be an annuity stream of income to be expected from year to year from a stable client base. We'll address each of these issues briefly.

Good Enough

"Good enough" may be good enough for you, but often, it is not good enough for potential buyers, whether they're from inside the practice or outside of it. To justify buying a practice, the buyer needs to see an opportunity to pay for it out of ongoing cash flow. The lower the net income and cash flow, the less value the buyer will see in it. In fact, if it's too low, a seller can count on having a difficult time even selling it. So if you are trying to maximize the value of your firm, start looking at "good enough" from the standpoint of the marketplace rather than just what is acceptable for you.

Not Within Your Control

There are always opportunities to make at least some incremental improvements that can add up to significant changes in the long run. What we find, under the surface of this comment, is that the changes that are needed or being contemplated are not easy, seem too risky, are uncomfortable, or would create conflict. If you are stuck as an owner in a business over which you have little influence, then the question is, why don't you just go to work for someone else? Our profession is at full employment, so you should have a ton of options. What we find is that "not within my control" is often a smoke screen to rationalize doing nothing because it is the easiest course of action to take. If you are an owner, you have influence and control. Use it to make the firm better; don't sit around hoping someone else will do that for you.

If you are expecting to sell out within a year or two, while you will still have time to address some of the ideas covered in this book, others will be more difficult, given that some changes will require too much ramp up time. So, do what you can, but starting taking action now!

Specialized Practices

Some specialized practices can yield a great deal of value when the owner decides to sell out. These are practices with deep specialty niches, often by market segment, that are leveraged through a cadre of talented professional staff, such as a specialty in, for example, auto dealers or construction contractors. On the other hand, a practice in which most of the work is done in the form of one-time projects, with little, if any, ongoing relationship with the client for repeat services, will be of lesser value. This should be obvious when you consider the fact that types of work such as business valuation and litigation support have to be resold continually inasmuch as there are no annuity relationships generally developed, except through various professional referral sources. It's worth even less if those referral sources are tied only to the departing owner.

The key here is to know what you are building and why. If you are just trying to build a practice because you like to do that kind of work, then great. Make money doing it, knowing that it might have a limited value when you are ready to retire. But if your objective is to build your specialized services to create value and income both today and in the future, do it in a way that allows others to be involved so that your practice has the best chance of sustaining itself beyond just you.

Charge Clients a Fair Fee

A key element to creating a robust overall profit stream is charging a fair fee for your work. It sounds really simple and straightforward, but the smaller the client we work with, the more this principle is abused. Most of our CPAs across the country give away too much of their time. Most of them charge far too little for the talent they bring to the table and for the risk they are assuming. From coast to coast, we hear "You don't understand our market area," or "We are in a small town," and so on. But consider this example.

> If you have a manager who makes $80,000 a year, you probably would expect that person to bill about $200,000 to make that salary work, which would require somewhere between 1,400 to 1,600 charge hours. Using this approach, you're going to need to be charging about $140–$150 an hour in order for that $80,000 a year manager to be able to bill at a level that justifies the salary being paid. If you are charging $140–$150 an hour for that manager, there also needs to be a substantial gap between the manager's hourly charge versus the partners' rates, or the firm will be motivating the clients to want to have the partners do all of the work. We are also assuming the partner makes more than $80,000 a year, which is another reason his or her rate needs to be higher—to reflect a rate that's reasonable for what the partner gets paid.

There are a number of problems with this scenario that we find in the marketplace:

- First, partners all over the country are not charging nearly enough for their time—if they don't charge enough for their time, you can assume that they are also charging too little for everyone else's time.

- Second, if a firm needs to be charging $150 an hour for the manager, the firm certainly doesn't want to charge $175 for a partner. As mentioned previously, everyone will want to stipulate that the partner do all the work if they can access that level of talent for only $25 more an hour.

- Third, when it comes time to sell or merge, it is important that the firm is charging close to market rates or higher because the firm is less valuable and less desirable if it is not. Transitioning clients is hard enough without adding the difficulty of having to substantially raise rates at the same time.

- Fourth, every market has a built-in balancing system when it comes to rates. For example, if in your market, you can get a manager with the same amount of expertise for $65,000 instead of $85,000, then that same ratio of billings to pay would simply apply against the $65,000 salary. This would mean that the manager would need to bill a little over $160,000, and at that same 1,500 charge hours would drive a charge rate of about $110. We have a billing worksheet in volume 2 to help you work through all of this depending on level of staff and compensation, but for now, the point is that we have not been in a market where the firm has to pay $80,000 but can only bill that person's time as if they were paid $65,000. In every market, the buy price (what you pay your employees) drives the sell price (their hourly charge rate), and they stay in balance. So if you claim that you have to pay high wages in your market, but you can't charge a proportionate rate for their time, it is only because you choose not to. We haven't seen those dynamics in any marketplace, regardless of how remote and rural.

A corollary to this principle is to make sure that you and your people are recording all of their time. You may decide later on to discount it. That's okay. But, record all of your time. When you're on the phone with the client, just talking to them for 5 or 10 minutes, it is common for a CPA to think they aren't going to bill for that and not bother entering the time spent into their time-keeping system. But 15 times a day over a 15-day period with the same client, for example, adds up. You can't afford to give away that kind of time. You are teaching the client that making quick calls to you is free, and you can rest assured they are smart, will catch on, and take advantage of you.

Track all your time with the understanding that you are not committing to do anything with it, except to look at it later on and make a billing decision then. Think about how much time starts to add up in these little 15-minute increments. Of any group in the world that understands this, CPAs should, so, we repeat:

Record all of your time.

If, at the end of the month, it adds up to only 15–30 minutes, if you don't wish to, you don't have to bill it. Better yet, show it on the invoice and then note that you're providing them a special client discount, or note what it was that you talked about and show it at "no charge." This builds client loyalty.

What probably will happen when you begin to record all your time is that about half of the time, you will look at an accumulation of time and realize that you spent three or four hours with that client, two or three with this client, and five or six with another. When you start adding it up, it is thousands and thousands of dollars that you are throwing away every month.

As well, stop giving away work, discounting work, and just bringing in work to keep people busy. This sets up a bad model. We're not saying that a couple times a year in the slowest periods that you might not take on some work at a reduced rate. The problem that we often see is that work doesn't stay in the slow season. It starts shifting into the busier time. You might be thinking that this work at least provides revenue, and it pays some bills. However, at some point, it distracts you from spending time with your better clients. Because you constantly stay busy, oftentimes doing low value work, you don't use your free time for getting in front of your top clients; doing one-on-one coaching, development, and training with key people that report to you; making sure you implement changes in the firm, and so on. You get stuck, and the firm starts to stagnate.

When you buy into the philosophy that all additional business sold, regardless of discount, is of value because it is additional revenue, you will quickly find that you are working much harder than ever before without much money to show for it. Don't be afraid of free time for you and your people during slow periods; there are far more valuable activities for everyone to accomplish than completing deeply discounted projects.

This same philosophy about avoiding the temptation to bring in discounted work during the slow periods applies to holding on to marginally profitable clients in any period. Don't be afraid to run them off. Bad clients are bad business; let them go. This gives you more time to spend with clients who *want* to pay you. If you are like every CPA firm we have worked with, you have clients right now that want to hire you to do more work for them, but you are always busy, and you don't talk to them unless they call. Don't let your bad clients suck the life out of you—let them go and spend more time with your good ones. When it comes time to retire, those marginal clients still won't provide you with any revenue because your internal or external buyer will run them off rather than pay you for them.

To clarify a point: you can terminate bad clients simply by raising their rates to the place that they deserve. Of course, if they're truly a bad client and they treat your people badly or they treat you badly, then get rid of them. But most of the time, bad clients are clients who don't want to pay you fair value for the work you are doing. Raise your rates to what they should be on the clients' work.

Our experience across the country is the same in cities as in rural areas. About 50 percent of them (and often, a lot more) will pay the larger fee, and they won't go anywhere. Even if you let 50 percent of them go, the additional margin you create from raising your rates to the proper level typically allows you to make the same amount of money or more with only half the time invested.

Another idea to consider in this context is using multiple billing rates. It is one thing to have a billing rate for tax preparation services, for instance. You literally are lining up work, picking up a folder, processing it, finishing it up, and going on to the next. You have something of an assembly line in place. You can be very productive that way, and a standard billing rate works fine when you can be that productive and efficient.

On the other hand, when you charge that same billing rate all the time, especially when the work you are doing doesn't allow that same level of utilization—like special project work—it will end up becoming a problem for you. This is because anytime you're doing special project work, you have to get up to speed, figure out where you are, talk with people, set up schedules, and interact with people in a different way. Now it's not just you in your office, picking up folder after folder. You're interacting with the world, and when you start interacting with the world, it is sloppy and inefficient and, therefore, you can't do it for the same rates. The billing rates we typically see in firms are the assembly-line work (that is, audits and tax returns) billing rates because much of the work they do is that kind of work. But when carrying out other types of projects, that rate doesn't make much sense because it doesn't account for all the other factors of lost time, start-up time, and so on. Consider creating multiple billing rates for each person based on the kind of work they are doing and its natural, built-in inefficiencies.

Manage Through the Trough

Almost every firm makes a lot of money during tax season—it is a key time to optimize your overall profit stream. However, many will spend the rest of the year trying to give that profit away. There are peaks and valleys in almost every business, and certainly in the business of public accounting. It is while in the valleys that firms tend to lose the profitability built up in busy season and other peak times. Don't give up your hard-earned profits in the trough—look at some options to allow you to further optimize your overall profit stream. Consider tactics such as hiring temporary help so when you finish that peak season, you can let them go or cut back on their hours, maintaining an appropriate staffing level for the trough. Take a look at accelerating some of the year-end analysis work that is going to have to be done to get the work finished in the busy season anyway—move it up and get a head start on it.

You might want to look at some of your weaker clients who aren't as profitable and push them out beyond the busy season into the trough. You are not making as much money on them, so push them out, extend their deadlines, or bring some work in early so that you can manage the next peak. Consider either offering discounts to some clients for allowing you to extend their work or giving them a choice that makes them feel like they're getting a discount. You can let them know that you're already discounting your fees below normal rates, and if you were charging normal rates, their work would cost $XXX more. Therefore, you're giving them a choice. You can either charge them something closer to what your standard fees are, or you can just push their work back a little bit and keep doing it for about the same price you have been doing it. Now at least they feel as though they're getting that discount.

Generally speaking, the people who you are moving into the trough are less pristine or are not your best clients. This type of tactic creates more time for you to spend with your good clients as their most trusted business adviser, acting as their general business consultant, building loyalty, and increasing profits—theirs and yours. Your good clients ought to be managed 12 months a year the best you can.

Another option is to get people to take vacation time, study for the CPA exam, spend time doing some quality training so that your people can take their skills to the next level, shadow partners to learn how to better interact with clients, be involved in implementing firm strategic goals, develop others that report to them, networking, participating in firm marketing activities, and so on. The list of activities your people can do during the trough that will make the firm better, faster, and stronger is almost infinite, yet many firms tend to choose the one option that will give them the most limited payback—doing marginally profitable work. Ultimately, how much money you make for the year often will come down to how well you manage the peaks and the valleys. So, manage the trough smartly.

In Conclusion

This chapter provided just a few ideas about how you can drive more money to the bottom line and build greater value in the firm. There are more ideas and more behind these ideas, as well as how to implement the various ideas, in volume 2. This chapter can best be summarized by the phrase, "Start running your firm like a business."

The good news is that public accounting and other personal service businesses, regardless of business model chosen, are pretty basic when it comes to identifying key performance drivers. The bad news for many firms is that they haven't been actively monitoring key performance metrics and managing their firm as assertively as they could be, or should be. With the skills that CPAs possess, beefing up operational reporting should be carried out fairly easily. However, it will take more effort in multi-owner practices to be certain that changes indicated through the routine monitoring and reporting systems actually occur. We'll give you some ideas on how to make that happen in chapter 6, which deals with governance, and chapter 15 on compensation and accountability.

Chapter 4: Identify and Describe Your Business Model

Eat What You Kill Versus Building a Village

CPA firms, generally speaking, look to one of two strategies to build and operate their firm. The first of these is what we call the Eat What You Kill (EWYK) model, and the second is the Building a Village model (BAV, more commonly called the One-Firm Concept model). When a CPA firm first opens its doors, the default model for start-ups and small operations is the EWYK model, which can be described as the model that places a premium on the superstars within the firm (those people who have extraordinary capability, commitment, aggressiveness, entrepreneurism, and stamina) for its current and future success. This model is very efficient, effective, and profitable because it places the burden of performance on a specific few with the expectation that they will be involved in every aspect of the business and in every decision made.

The second model, BAV, is just the opposite. It can be described as a model that places a premium on people who operate the firm and create and follow systems, processes, and procedures, with a methodology (infrastructure) to maximize the potential of all the people that work within it, not just the superstars. Table 4-1 lists some differences between the two models.

Both models are important to building and developing a successful service operation, but the optimum profile differs depending on the maturity of the firm. In other words, needing to move to the BAV model is usually a function of enormous success from operating under the EWYK model. Start-up CPA firms are usually founded on the superstar philosophy, which relies on an individual or two to find the clients, service them, bill and collect, and, in their spare time, run the business. Without these entrepreneurs, there would be no business to transition because the superstar strategy is so dependent on these individuals, successful transition is tricky. As a firm matures and the demand for services becomes more consistent and predictable, an operator management strategy becomes more effective. This operator mentality shifts the firm's

Table 4-1

EWYK—Superstars	BAV—Operators
Look for extraordinary employees to leverage the firm's processes.	Look to extraordinary processes to leverage the firm's employees.
Believe that the perpetuation of the firm and its future success is heavily dependent on a specific person who is a natural leader at the helm.	Believe the firm's future success is less about a specific person and more about a strong infrastructure in place, with clearly defined roles and responsibilities for the leaders to follow.
Place a premium on adding self-starter, entrepreneurially minded personalities to the organization (people who are business developers with strong, take-charge personalities) to sustain the growth of a business.	Place a premium on talented people with great attitudes who can be taught the skills they need through the firm's training and development processes and can be developed into the leaders the firm is looking for.
Believe that *the cream will rise to the top on its own* or have an *only-the-strong-will-survive* attitude about development, and believe that those people (the strong) instinctively know what competencies are important and should be developed.	Believe that almost anyone can develop into a technically competent project manager with client relationship responsibility; therefore, believe that people development is about establishing competency expectations at every level within a defined career path and then spending the necessary time and effort training and monitoring performance and holding people accountable to living up to those expectations.
Thrive on creating, changing, inventing, experimenting, and taking risks.	Thrive on consistency, controls, setting standards, compliance with standards, continuous improvement, and managing risk.
Believe that the success of the firm is less important than the personal relationships he or she maintains with his or her clients.	Believe that individual partners' clients are less important than the values and strategies of the firm.
Believe that he or she is entitled to have a say in every aspect of the way the business is run.	Believe that the partners should set strategy, process, policy, and budgets and then leave the implementation of those directives to management.
Believe success for the organization is best achieved by he or she building their book or improving their book's profitability.	Believe that success for the organization is best achieved through better management of resources for growth and profitability of the whole firm as a whole.

culture away from catering to irreplaceable people to developing an infrastructure that creates irreplaceable positions (that a variety of people can successfully fill). A few basic principles of an operator model are as follows:

- Developing leadership that can successfully function within the existing structure so that the firm's success will continue.
- Creating a viable and enduring chain of command with clearly understood and adhered to roles and responsibilities. This allows a structure that supports new people filling important positions, functioning within a range of known powers and limitations.
- Operating like a firm rather than like a group of individual partners. The firm controls who serves the clients, what services are offered, and what processes and procedures are followed—not the individual CPAs managing the relationships.

- Transitioning of clients occurs any time the firm decides a client could be better served by other resources (for example, if the skill set of an individual more closely matches the services utilized by that client) or in order to balance the distribution of demand among resources (partners with huge differences in books managed).
- Developing systems to reward desired behavior and discourage undesired behavior. These systems are built to reflect the current firm strategy, are usually based on both objective and subjective criteria, reward overachievement, put a spotlight on underachievement, and are put in place to raise the firm's minimum standard of performance.
- Developing a staffing model that leverages work (continually pushes work down) and is based on everyone at each level producing at or above the minimum level expected for each identified competency. In other words, this model expects people to perform at or above minimum competency levels for all defined competencies rather than be exceptional at a few with other competencies being nonexistent.

Viewed another way, the EWYK model places an emphasis on the superstar as a natural hunter. These hunters go out and start a new business (create a village). Because there are few members of the village, these natural hunters are involved in everything, from hunting, to skinning, to food preparation, to clean-up (because of the typical hunter's strong personality and entrepreneurial spirit, the hunter believes he or she is better at all of those things than everyone else). As the village thrives, there is continued stress on the hunters to get everything done and meet the growing demands from the village.

When the hunters realize they need to get more accomplished, they think about getting others involved in the village to assist them. The focus is on making the few hunters—their most scarce resource—more productive. A hunter might ask, "I need to go out and kill more game, so how can I get others involved to support me?" To answer, let's expand on this analogy. Let's say that the hunter is a bow hunter. The hunter might think, "Let's assign someone from the village to carry my quivers full of arrows. I can move faster along the ground and save energy because I am not carrying as much weight." This added support instantly creates additional efficiency and effectiveness.

But at some point, the demands of the village continue to grow, and the hunter has to consider other approaches to being more productive. The next idea might be to bring a couple of people from the village along on the hunts to collect all the dead game and guard this food source until later in the day, when the hunter can come back and skin all the meat at one time. Once again, this change creates efficiency of the hunters' time.

The message from this analogy is to drive home the point that when the typical entrepreneur thinks about expanding, he or she thinks about ways to leverage himself or herself. Remember what we said previously: without that person taking this approach, there probably would be no business to grow to the point of becoming successful. But as the village continues to grow, at some point, the stress under this model causes the firm to implode because it is all about people sitting around waiting to be helpful to the superstars. The helpers become less and less efficient because there is more and more waiting on the superstars to do what they need to do, and the superstars finally get to a point where there are no more hours left to work.

On the other hand, the BAV model focuses on making the most out of the talent within the village. It is no longer just about the hunter. There comes a point when we start focusing on specialization because we realize the difficulty of teaching someone how to do everything the hunters do so well. Instead, we focus on teaching someone to do just one thing well and taking that function away from the hunter. Under the BAV approach, people in the village take on more and more activities so that they can constantly narrow the role of the hunter and remove him or her from as many processes as possible. For example, leaders teach others to skin the game, and because that is all the skinners do, they become very proficient at it very quickly. In order to teach people how to perform specialized processes and avoid creating another hunter situation, leaders combine this instruction with more processes, support, methodology, and infrastructure to allow the talent within the village to flourish more quickly. If someone gets hurt and can't perform that function, we just pick someone else in the village to follow the roadmap that was built to teach the skinners how to skin each type of game to deliver the maximum amount of quality meat for the village.

The hunters will always be important to the firm, but by using this approach, we constantly narrow their roles and responsibilities so they become easier to replace. Pretty soon, the hunter might be cut out of every process but hunting. Because of the constant development of talent within the village, the hunter may even be directed to only kill certain types of game for the village in order to create opportunity for villagers to start learning how to hunt the game that requires less experience.

To make this clear, we want superstars. We want hunters in our organization. But there comes a time when it is too difficult to train someone to do everything: being a skilled hunter, skinner, food preparer, and so on. It's important to remember that the entrepreneur had a unique training ground. There was virtually no one else to do those jobs, so entrepreneurs became proficient at doing them out of necessity, at a time when the volume and complexity of the business was much less. But given the new level of success and volume of the business, it makes a lot more sense to narrow what you want people to learn and provide them with enough of that work so that they can become proficient in their specialty area very quickly.

The Problem With Replacing the Superstar

Someone who comes from an EWYK background whose business is growing will look for hunters who are just as good at the following:

- Business development
- Handling technical issues
- Being a visionary
- Assessing and assuming reasonable risks comfortably, and so much more.

The fact is, it is almost impossible to find that particular skills package, and if the person with the EWYK background does find it, it is because they met someone running their own firm (or possibly worse, someone who wants to come on board for a short time to get to know people in the area so they can leave and start their own firm).

As long as a firm continues to grow with a superstar or a couple of superstars and those people have plenty of capability and capacity left, then the firm is in a good position. But once a superstar's capacity is used up in this model, then for the firm to grow, they have to find additional superstars. Because superstar is the least practical and least likely position to fill in an organization, firms typically grow until the original superstars in the firm are at maximum capacity. Because of the flat organizational structure they have built and because of the firm's dependence on those superstars to perform the major functions of the organization, the firm's growth quickly stagnates at that point.

The BAV model basically shifts the focus to roles and responsibilities away from just personalities so people with a modicum of common sense, intelligence, and training could come in and become successful in that environment. Because of the leverage this approach takes, superstars can narrow their focus to one of their most important functions within the firm—to manage client and referral relationships—and be able to double and even triple the current client load they have due to their diffused focus. This allows the firm to easily start growing again as well as to create greater opportunities for all the newly minted talent they have acquired and developed.

Modes of Operation Within the EWYK and BAV Models

To help you consider the evolution from EWYK to BAV, we identified a model of how a firm might evolve from one model to the other, which we call Modes of Operation (illustrated in Figure 4-1). Within the EWYK and BAV models, there are some logical steps through which firms migrate. We broke this down into four basic modes: the Survival Mode, the Safety Mode, the Success Mode, and the Continuation Mode. None of these are bad. We simply find that, as we are introduced to firms at all stages of their evolution, there are differing areas of focus as well as different approaches to help firms move from one level to the next.

While this is the common evolutionary path in the success of a firm, sometimes firms will skip a step in the cycle. They don't all start at the beginning of the cycle, either. Regardless, we still find it helpful when we take our first look at a firm to see at what step they are likely operating so that we have a better insight about likely obstacles and opportunities they will be facing or addressing in the near term.

Figure 4-1

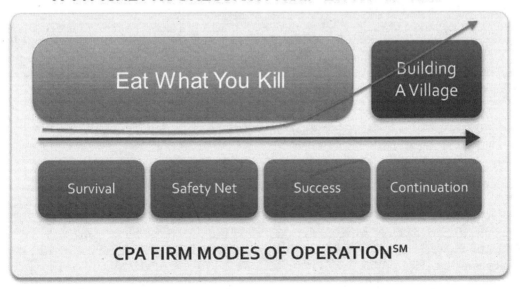

A TYPICAL PROGRESSION FROM "EWYK" to "BAV"

Eat What You Kill

Building A Village

Survival Safety Net Success Continuation

CPA FIRM MODES OF OPERATION[SM]

Survival Mode

The very first mode of operation is Survival Mode. As the name indicates, it's about the survival of the firm. It's about finding clients, finding projects, selling the work, billing it, collecting it, and getting enough work and volume completed and collected so that there's money to pay the overhead. Simply put, it is the start-up phase of putting meat and potatoes on the table. In this mode, you are trying to get to the point that you can feel like you're covering your costs and able to take out enough personally so that you can stop feeling like you are living paycheck to paycheck. Typically, one of the big characteristics of Survival Mode, as you might imagine, is that it's predominantly based on the production and the work effort of the owner or owners of the firm because there may not be any other employees. In this mode, the focus is on doing whatever it takes to keep the firm operational so that the owner can continue to work for the firm rather than become an employee in some other organization.

Safety Net Mode

When a firm moves to Safety Net Mode, there is enough money coming in that it is no longer an issue whether the firm will survive. It is no longer a day-to-day issue to pay the bills or provide the partners a reasonable amount of pay. Now the focus turns to paying off firm debt, paying off individual debt, and creating both firm and individual surpluses to build up some financial reserves. This mode is about starting to build an organization that's strong enough to give greater financial security to the partners. Like in Survival Mode, the greatest amount of work is being done by the partners in Safety Net Mode, but the firm might have brought in some people by this time to help leverage the partners' particular skills and time. To continue the village metaphor, in this mode, the hunter decides to have someone carry the quivers full of arrows or guard the game in one spot so the hunter can efficiently skin them all later.

Success Mode

By the time they get to Success Mode, the partners are starting to think of the firm as something to protect (the entity needs to survive, not just the partners). The focus changes to create a culture that attracts more people so the firm becomes a nicer, kinder, more flexible place to work. It is at this stage that the firm might want to be the employer of choice or make it into a top list of places to work. Often, at this level, the firm will begin to focus on its core philosophy, values, and strategy. By this time, there are far more people than just the partners producing revenue, but the driving mentality is still rooted in creating positions around the specific skills and personality strengths of the partners while enhancing the image and efficiency of the firm.

It's important to note at this success level that we're not talking about the firm having an institutional identity. Certainly, there might be an effort to have an identity, but within the firm and to the marketplace, the identity of and the loyalty to the organization is attached to the individual partners.

It is in Success Mode that many of the BAV processes, training, and methodology are installed, creating a hybrid model. However, a reasonable percentage of processes and thinking continue from the EWYK model. This is the stage where roles and responsibilities are created, mentors are assigned, and leadership positions are formalized, but with little to no teeth behind creating the necessary accountability to make those positions truly effective. The conflict in this hybrid is that the EWYK model leaves the power and accountability in the hands of the superstars to individually decide how their efforts are going to drive their firm's success, while the BAV model puts the power in the hands of the organizational structure to achieve the same goal, which requires the superstars to become accountable to the firm instead of just themselves. Some version of the Success Mode hybrid is where we find most firms above $2 million and below $30 million in revenues.

Continuation Mode

Continuation Mode is basically creating a firm that has its own institutional identity. In other words, when clients think about the firm, they don't think about the partners first and the firm second, but the other way around: the firm first, with the partners simply being the expected talent within such a reputable organization. In this mode, the focus shifts to looking at processes and procedures so they make sense for any group of partners rather than just the current ones in power. For example, when we are working with firms and talking about how they operate, they normally defend their current operating structure and processes vigilantly and vehemently as being of the BAV variety. However, when we ask "So, how effective would this be, and how supportive would you be, if you were removed from the current positions you hold and some other partner would take your place?", almost 100 percent of the time, the answer we get is, "No, I would not support running the firm that way if I were not in the position I am in today." What this reveals is that they're still operating at the margins between Success and Continuation Modes.

In Continuation Mode, the focus shifts to running the firm in a way that can be equally effective for both current and future partners. This means that the firm will shift to operating under an infrastructure and an organization that transcends any specific partner. The firm will create governance and decision-making processes geared to help create a culture that puts the entity first rather than the partners first. What is different in Continuation Mode is that instead of generating work and building roles and responsibilities around the specific strengths of partners, the partners generate work the firm has decided it wants through strategy. The firm designs roles and responsibilities for positions within the firm that people are asked to fill. There's a clear emphasis with this mode on creating replicability and interchangeable parts. There is also a focus on training and developing people to make the entire team better, faster, and stronger rather than just making a superstar or two better, faster, and stronger; so by this point, the firm truly is operating as one firm. The partners realize that their organization is no longer about them, but about their need to protect the firm and the people who work within it.

A good way to apply this outside of our profession is to think about sports teams that seem to constantly get to postseason playoffs. Think about the teams that throughout the year have injured superstars, yet the team doesn't miss a beat because their replacements step up and fill the missing roles. This doesn't happen magically or because certain teams are lucky and have more talent than everyone else. It happens because these unique teams, operating under the interchangeable parts philosophy, don't ask their people to "be" and "do" everything; rather, they ask their team members to fill a narrowly defined role and do that well. This allows people to step up and fill gaps much more quickly, efficiently, and effectively, which is a foundational principle of Continuation Mode.

The Most Commonly Found Disconnect

The most commonly found disconnect is between Success and Continuation Modes. It is not always clear whether a firm is still operating predominantly in Success or Continuation Mode. At first glance, it is common to see a firm that has a good

- training program for staff,
- partner-in-training program,
- recruiting process,
- commitment to technology,
- systems for marketing, and more.

The thought that quickly comes to mind is, "Wow, they're operating in Continuation Mode and doing a great job!" But when you start looking at how the firm operates, you find that while the organization clearly invests in all of these important processes, the real nucleus of the firm comes down to five or six partners who run the business. Everything still centers on these partners' client books of business, and they are paid based on that entitlement rather than what they are doing to achieve the firm's current strategy. When these partners are out selling, although they talk about the firm, the conversation still boils down to a commitment from "me"—an individual partner—rather than "me" backed by the full weight and reputation of the firm.

When firms try to make the transition between EWYK and BAV or the "One Firm Concept," the most common scenario is a firm outwardly operating in Continuation Mode, but internally, their roots are still strongly connected to Success Mode. Visually described, although a firm might have a toe, or even a leg, in Continuation Mode, their support leg and torso are still lingering back in Success Mode, where there is comfort in the firm still catering to the partner, his or her clients, and his or her desires. It is rare to find firms that holistically operate in Continuation Mode until they become some of the very largest firms in our profession. Most firms with 50 full-time equivalents (FTEs) or greater either function heavily in Success Mode with some part of their operations in Continuation Mode, or they have a large portion of their operations in Continuation Mode but still have a strong foothold back in Success Mode. This distinction tends to be most clear in compensation models. When the compensation models are all about partner production and partner clients rather than firm goals and firm clients, we have found that these firms are rooted in Success Mode, and until those roots are severed, that is where they will stay.

Modes of Operation Summary

Survival Mode. In the initial stages of being an entrepreneur, we are driven by the instinct to pay for the roof over our heads and put food on the table.

Safety Net Mode. Once we feel like our business will generate the resources required to cover our basic needs, we focus on building the business to generate enough cash that we can build a fat savings account, pay off our business notes, and create a cushion in case times get tough.

Success Mode. Now that we don't feel desperate about our financial security, we start thinking about evolving our firm in a way that makes the partners and the people we are hiring want to work there. Additionally, the firm becomes an entity we think about protecting. The firm's success, reputation, and strengths still are reflective and synonymous with those of the partners in this mode.

Continuation Mode. At this point, our focus shifts from our success (when the partners have done well financially and are secure in their own accomplishments) to creating an organization that has its own institutional identity and can survive without the partners.

Important Distinctions Between the EWYK and BAV Models

The first distinction that comes to mind is the difference between how partners look at their role in the firm. In an EWYK model, it's about my book, my clients, my people, my strategy, my goals, my policies, and what I want to do. In a BAV model, it's about the firm's clients, the firm's policies, the firm's people, and the firm's strategy that I'm going to support.

A foundational principle regarding the BAV model is developing leadership throughout the organization. The firm has to prioritize creating and sustaining a viable and enduring chain of command that will allow the firm to continue to grow and develop beyond any of its current leaders. Building a village is about developing systems to reward desired behavior. In other words, the firm is paying people to focus on the firm rather than paying people to focus on themselves as individual partners. It's about developing a culture that focuses on developing people and closing competency gaps at every level.

It's also about making everybody stronger, not just the partners. A key to doing this is grooming replacements. It is everyone's job to groom their replacements. Without a replacement, everyone will get stuck in their current role. No one can do two jobs, so if somebody is going to step into a new role and they haven't developed their replacement, they're in trouble. Experience says that the newly promoted person is going to be expected to fill the higher role (the one he or she was just promoted to), but not have the capacity to actually perform that role because of all the time that will be required to be allocated to the undone tasks in the lower role. This usually results in the newbie performing poorly after being promoted. The newbie's management commonly loses confidence in them during this transition, not because the newbie isn't working hard but because he or she is still tethered to their old role (which, by the way, is actually the fault of management; however, management rarely sees it that way).

Here is a common scenario about building the right capacity within the firm. Under an EWYK model, a partner might have two or three go-to people they use to get their work done. When the firm wants to recruit and spend money to hire and implement elaborate training processes, the EWYK partner sits in the partner meeting thinking about his or her own book and his or her own go-to people, and says, "We don't need to spend all of that time and money because I don't need anyone else. Hiring more people is just wasting my money. If you want to hire more people so that you can build your book, then you should hire them, and they should come out of your pocket."

Unfortunately, in the EWYK model, growth goes to a partner and usually benefits, for the most part, a partner. Therefore, hiring people is not seen as anything the firm should invest in, it's just viewed as small incremental additions of capacity needed to handle client demand or when partners are shorthanded. But, by the time this happens, the firm is way behind the eight ball because partners need bodies for work that is already in-house and often behind schedule. So, staffing for growth and building the right capacity for an EWYK firm is riddled with obstacles.

Another area of conflict with best practices that occurs more frequently with EWYK firms is that of promoting managers to partners before the managers demonstrate partner-level competencies. For example, a big-booked partner in an EWYK firm will become very motivated to bring in his or her go-to manager as partner as soon as that partner feels like his or her book would be at risk if that manager left the firm. Put another way, once a manager becomes too important to the day-to-day project management of a partner's book, then that partner will try to promote that manager in order to lock him or her into the firm.

EWYK firms tend to rarely have enough capacity to get their work done without the partners all putting in 2,600 hours of work or more because of the staffing issues mentioned previously. This constant shortage of capacity as well as the siloed nature of the firm model makes it common to find many partners functioning as managers, but who were only made partners as part of a damage control strategy by one of the senior partners to protect his or her book. As long as there are no major leadership changes within the firm, having partners who act like managers isn't a big deal; but it will certainly become a big deal when leadership starts to change and as the firm puts together its succession strategy.

Under the BAV model, this situation is less likely to occur because partners submit work to a pool of people, not one go-to person. Work is performed as talent becomes available, not queued up for a specific person. Therefore, when someone is promoted to partner under this model, it is because he or she has obtained expected competencies, an opportunity for a partner position opened up, or that person was deemed a good fit for the firm, not because of the risk of possible economic loss to one partner.

Another big difference is that "Book is king." "Book" is where power, influence, and privilege emanate from in an EWYK firm. For example, most EWYK firms don't even think about their ownership or equity interest in the firm because their compensation and vote is based on the size of their book more than on their ownership. In the BAV model, it doesn't work that way. As soon as a partner starts pounding his or her chest and making demands because of book size, the rest of the partners turn to the managing partner and suggest that it is time to move some of the clients of the chest-pounding partner to other partners.

Probably the biggest organizational difference between the EWYK and BAV models is accountability. When the clients are yours and what you earn from those clients is predominantly yours, how can a partner group demand that a partner follow specific policies? The superstar partner will say, "I understand why we have those policies, but they don't apply to my clients. It doesn't matter if I collect my accounts receivable (A/R) as fast as another partner because my collections offset my earnings. If my timesheets are not done on time, then I don't make as much money as I could." In other words, the typical EWYK partner compensation system is so closely tied with the partner's earnings that he or she usually gets instantly rewarded or punished for their behavior.

Because we can already hear what is going through your mind, let us say, no, there is very limited to no accountability in this model because we are talking about accountability to the firm, not accountability to personal earnings.

There are bushels full of examples of partners acting inappropriately as a partner in a firm, even though he or she is financially punished for his or her behavior.

- Consider a partner billing only once every six months. Although they might not get a draw for their salaries, the firm still has to cover all the other salaries and overhead.
- Along those same lines, what about partners that won't collect their A/R and have average balances of 150 days or more?
- Consider partners that treat staff rudely, motivating some of your best people to quit.
- What about partners that put their work in front of everyone else's, even though the work going to the front of the queue could easily be pushing "A" client work behind "C" client work just to appease a bullying partner?
- What about cross-selling? Consider a client who needs a service the firm offers, but to whom the partner who owns the client book won't make the introduction because he or she doesn't want to.
- Consider clients that treat your staff horribly. This is one of the few circumstances in which we simply say, "Fire those clients!" But we can tell you from experience that those clients won't be fired because they are a part of a partner book of business, which is where that partner draws his or her pay and power.
- What about a client acceptance problem caused by a partner bringing in a new client at a price way below standard during peak season when the firm has no available resources?

We could go on and on. The point is that in the EWYK model, partners are accountable to their earnings, but not to the firm. In the BAV model, partners are first accountable to the firm, then accountable for their contribution to the firm, which is reflected in their earnings.

In Conclusion

When we talk about the EWYK model, we are talking about silos within a firm and how they can share overhead and operate within just enough rules to keep the group from splitting up and going their separate ways. It is like having separate firms sharing the same name in order to have the critical mass to afford necessary resources. There is nothing wrong with this model, and, as we said at the beginning of this chapter, it is the way almost all businesses start up. But at some point in the process, the firm becomes successful enough and employs enough people that it outgrows this business model; or just as likely, silos disagree about the appropriateness of certain rules and split off because the pain of operating together becomes greater than the need for autonomy.

Many times, siloed firms never really have to face the problem of outgrowing their business model because one of two common scenarios occurs. In the first scenario, rather than find a way to pull all the silos into one firm, various silos spin off from time to time as the firm gets bigger, which resizes the multiple new entities so they are small enough to be acceptable with the EWYK model. In the second scenario, the firm stagnates and stops growing. Although some partners might want to continue growing the firm, the pain of changing to a new, unproven model is deemed too risky and uncomfortable than just living with the stagnation.

We want to make one point very clear: both models are important, both models work, and there are successful examples of each all over the country. The BAV model has to be put in place most often because of the enormous success of the EWYK model, not because of some failing. But as you can tell from the preceding narrative, far more money and time is invested in the firm's infrastructure in the BAV (operator) model than in the EWYK (superstar) model. "Hunters" commonly equate more people, more training, expected competencies, and greater amounts of time spent in management as unproductive. Even more importantly, they see these as unprofitable hours. However, based on a multitude of profession-wide practice management surveys, "more people and more training" clearly equates to "more money for the partners." For a superstar to make the BAV model work, he or she must be able to adopt a philosophy that likely is both unnatural and uncomfortable.

Our experience shows that the easiest path for smooth succession is in the BAV (operator) model. Although success may flourish in the superstar model, its succession strategy is dependent on finding incoming superstars to take over or outsiders to buy it up. This model is very limiting. It is hard for a firm to grow beyond about $3 million with the superstar philosophy, although we have seen firms grow to about $15 million (but to be fair, those firms are typically made up of many small offices that keep the silos separated and the conflicts typically more disguised). But there are plenty of EWYK firms with very happy partners that do exactly what they want to do. And to many, this total flexibility to build a firm that caters to each partner's personal whims is worth more than any retirement value. If that means they shut off the lights as they walk out the door on the day they retire, then so be it.

By now, it shouldn't surprise anyone that this book is about how to operate within whatever model you choose. For those who choose EWYK, we will give you plenty of guidance about how to structure your organization to maximize profitability as well as how to set up benefits consistent with the inner workings of the model. For those who want their firm to be able to survive multiple generations of partners and, therefore, choose to move from EWYK to BAV, or even more specifically, to move from Success Mode to Continuation Mode, we will discuss how to successfully bridge that gap, as well. Just recognize that whichever model you pick, you get a package deal of its benefits and detriments.

Chapter 5: Examine Retirement Benefits

The Nuances of a Fair Retirement Benefit

When we take our clients through succession planning, it doesn't take long for the conversation to turn to implementing the best practices for running the firm. But typically, before we can make any significant changes to the way the firm operates or partners are compensated, regardless of what the agreed-to best practice is, we normally begin by visiting retirement and associated benefits. Why? Because for big changes to occur, you usually need buy-in from a supermajority vote of the partner group, with the senior partners of the firm having a great influence—if not control—over the way that vote swings. For senior partners to be willing to take the risk that changing the firm will add value and greater success, they usually need some assurance that their risks are mitigated. A good way to mitigate some of those risks is to pin down the retirement process and benefits so that senior partners see the carrot dangling in front of them, making change far more palatable.

Our rule of thumb about a retiring partner is that the remaining partners in a firm may pay that retiring partner up to 120 percent of the fair market value of their ownership or book (depending on the operating model in place), and the partner selling his or her ownership or book may take as little as 80 percent of the fair market value to be willing to quietly step away from the firm. When either group goes even a hair outside this boundary (and often, even when they start coming close to it), then "principle" is invoked, and bad things begin to happen. The conversation shifts from one of win-win, when all parties come out okay, to win-lose, with each party out to hurt the other for being selfish and unfair.

Therefore, the first stake to put in the ground for building a succession plan is a fair retirement package. Generally, that is made up of two components: a return of capital and the retirement benefit. For EWYK firms, this equates to having a first right of refusal to buy the retiring partner's book. For BAV firms, it is about paying a benefit for the contribution that the retiring partner has made to the firm. This calculation often comes in the form of a multiple of salary or the partner's share of equity ownership applied to the net revenues of the firm.

Determining the Value

Based on the results of succession management surveys we've conducted with PCPS over the last dozen years, larger firms clearly favor the multiple of salary or the owner-ship times discounted net revenues approaches, while smaller firms tend to use the book of business method.

Our general rule of thumb is that if you are going to sell your book, it likely will be done based on a retention agreement paid out over four or five years, unless the sale is $200,000 in revenue or less because these firms will commonly sell with a much shorter payment cycle. So, although the agreed-upon purchase price would probably default to a $1 for $1 of revenue, given normal retention, the final payout to the selling partner over the payout period would likely be somewhere between 60–70 cents on the dollar (because the selling partner only gets paid for clients retained during each of their pay-ment years).

If you are using salary as your retirement benefit calculator, the most common multiplier we run across is 3 times total compensation based on the average of your 3 highest years' salary in the last 5 years to 10 years. Some firms will throw out the high and low figures when making this calculation. Some firms have moved to 2.5 times compensation because of the high compensation paid to its senior partners.

As for the ownership interest times net revenue approach, the most common discount we see is 15 cents on the dollar, resulting in a net benefit of around 85 cents on the dollar. The net annualized revenues (NAR) is usually calculated as an average of the last two years' revenue to reflect consistency of revenues as well as to ensure games are not played inflating (by the retiring partner) or deflating (by the firm) revenues in the final year before retirement. However, in this model, we recommend that you also subtract any outstanding debt owed to retired partners for their benefits (not outstanding loans to operate the business, just those amounts still due to partners who have sold their interest in the firm or debt owed due to merged-in firms). So, if you were a $5,000,000 firm with $1 million owed to a recently retired partner, and if the cur-rent retiring partner owned 20 percent of the firm, the calculation would be as follows:

Average NAR (assuming a two-year average)	$5,000,000
Less outstanding debt to retiring partners	1,000,000
Average NAR less retirement obligations	$4,000,000
Revenue adjustment	85¢ on the dollar
Equity interest of the retiring partner	20%
Retirement benefit ($4M × .85 × 20%)	$680,000

In this example, the 20-percent partner would be entitled to $680,000, usually paid out over 10 years, at no interest. While some firms pay out the benefit over 5–8 years, we most commonly find it to be 10 years.

In addition to the retirement benefit, an owner will receive a repayment of his or her capital. Simply put, if the firm is a partnership, then the accrual basis capital account is tracked and that amount is returned to the selling owner. In a corporate structure, the owner will receive his or her percentage of ownership multiplied by the accrual net book value of tangible assets. Thus, it is normally adjusted for what is believed to be collectable receivables, and billable or collectable work in progress, with a fair value assigned to the depreciated fixed assets. Because the liabilities associated with the deferred compensation obligations owed to retired owners are dealt with in our scenario in the value calculation, they would not be factored into the capital determination. Obviously, if we are talking about a sole proprietor selling his or her book of business, the sole proprietor keeps whatever cash is available after the dissolution of the company and its assets in addition to whatever is earned through the sale of the book. Capital is typically returned over three to five years (three years if the number is low, but commonly five years when that number is several hundred thousand dollars or more) at the firm's borrowing rate of interest.

Other Issues to Consider

Although the preceding section outlines the common starting places for retirement benefit calculations, there are variations. For example, interest or guarantees added to the retirement benefit usually end up with the retiring partners being paid a premium. If the benefits are set at something less than described previously, the odds are high that the retiring partner is getting less than market. But understand that in this chapter, we are only talking about this from the 10,000-foot level, not dealing with common quirks or dysfunction in a firm. Your numbers can vary significantly from what we have described previously and still be fair, depending on the entire package of perks.

For example, if the partner wants to continue working for the firm after his or her sale of ownership, how good or bad the terms of post-sale employment are will determine whether the entire retirement benefit is in line. Or, if a partner poorly transitions clients and the retirement benefit is not reduced for that infraction, then that can make a good deal bad, or what might have seemed like a bad deal for the seller turn good. Or, if 85 cents on the dollar is used to determine the benefit but the firm's revenues are tied to services that will not be offered after the partner retires, a lot of the client work is nonrecurring, or if much of the work is for services that are constantly up for rebidding with little loyalty in the process, then defining fair value as we did above is no longer fair.

The preceding information is just a starting place for this discussion, but in the end, it assumes predominantly recurring revenue, strong infrastructure (trained people), governance that will allow the firm to continue (in other words, a system in which the remaining partners can be held accountable to the firm's strategy), and so on. The assumption within the pricing we have covered for any deal other than "selling a book of business on retention" is that there is an organized firm with talent ready to profitably sustain it. We certainly wouldn't recommend someone "selling a book of business on retention" to any firm that doesn't meet this same set of criteria, but because we were singling out best practice retirement plans under the BAV model, we eliminated the EWYK retirement model in our previous explanation. To conclude, anything short of a sustainable, profitable firm means that adjustments need to be made to the best practice fair pricing we have been discussing.

We can't walk away from our conversation about over- and underpayment without adding this caveat: Probably 80 percent of senior partners would suggest that their firm will have a hard time remaining viable without them. The concern with what we just covered using the "sustainable, profitable firm" as the baseline is that this could be perceived as a free pass to every senior owner to sell the firm out from under its remaining partners, because they don't believe the firm will be sustainable and profitable after they leave. We have not given any such free pass. Our favorite phrase is "the fish stinks at the head": If you are one of the senior partners getting ready to retire and you haven't built anything sustainable, then shame on you. Know that you are one of the people who need to be taking a deep discount in your retirement benefits for the inadequacy of what you have built. If you have questions about the quality of the people and the organization you have created, then make the necessary investments in time and development and fix it before you leave. This act will not only create your legacy, but it will also justify you getting full benefits (not premium benefits, but full benefits).

Founding senior owners commonly have an entitlement perspective when it comes to retirement benefits. It starts with the philosophy of, "You [the remaining partners] wouldn't even have a firm to run and pay you so generously if it wasn't for me [retiring senior owner]." When this group looks at value, they view it from the perspective of what should be the value for all the partners, besides them, of course. Unfortunately, when it comes to the determination of retirement benefits for founding owners, it is fairly common for them to expect the standard retirement benefit plus some amount of founding father premium for creating the firm. This emotional time is further exacerbated by the fact that, in many cases, the founding owners also expect the remaining partners to voluntarily propose this idea of paying a premium benefit to pay homage and tribute to them for the bounty they have brought to the firm. The senior owners forget they have been the highest paid partners in the firm for years, and that many of the younger partners have been the workhorses for the firm for a decade or more while waiting for their turn to be the ones in charge. They forget that they, the senior owners, have commonly decided not to address important staffing or competency issues in order to maximize their pay in their later years or leave other key management issues unaddressed or unresolved.

So, while the younger partners typically wouldn't be in such a great position professionally without the help and mentorship of the senior partners, a key reason the firm commonly has many of its current succession and operational problems is because the senior partners were in control and didn't make the necessary investments in the firm to fix the problems. Maybe the fairest way to look at this is that the founding owners should get a premium for what they created and a big reduction for what they allowed to remain broken along the way.

Mandatory Sale of Ownership

This discussion addresses when someone has to retire. For the rest of this chapter, we will refer to this as *mandatory date of sale of ownership* (MSO).

Many senior owners want to continue working until they can't get out of bed to come to work anymore. Most of them also want to be paid their high salaries throughout that extended period, which often includes years of working a light schedule (or we could be more direct: working part-time as compared to the rest of the partners). After working with executives for over 30 years, we find that every one of them thinks they earn every penny of their compensation regardless of how much they make, and the vast majority feel that they are underpaid. So, don't expect an admission from a senior partner that they are overpaid. We have never seen it. Even when partners are working less than half-time and are still among the highest paid, they justify their compensation with statements like, "This firm wouldn't exist without me," "I brought these people in and they wouldn't have a job without me," or one of many other self-serving rationalizations.

Given that senior partners

- usually delegate more and more of their work to younger partners and managers, and unfortunately, more often to younger partners,
- often hoard book management and cap-out so they no longer contribute to firm growth because their book stagnates,
- commonly shift their thinking from growing, improving, and investing in the organization to maintaining the status quo and maximizing compensation, and
- have a more and more difficult time giving fair consideration to the demands and expectations of the youngest employees because of an age gap of more than four decades,

it is essential for a good succession plan to embrace a mandatory date of sale of ownership.

Based on our experience and the succession management surveys we've been conducting, firms are starting to change from MSO at age 65 to a partner being eligible to receive full retirement benefits at age 65 assuming 2 years' advance notice, with MSO at either 66 or 67 (with a very small number of firms setting the top age as a floating value established by Social Security).

MSO is usually the ugliest discussion of all when we work with firms, far uglier than the retirement benefit amount because it involves telling a senior partner, who takes pride in the business he or she has been part of building over the years, that he or she is no longer needed or wanted. A common response from one of the remaining partners might be, "That isn't the case; we are willing to create an agreement after MSO for them to continue to work." But in almost all the cases we see, MSO is a way to severely restrict a partner's daily impact and influence on the firm. There are two sides to being a partner. One is filling the role of partner, and the other is being a leader and having influence over decisions in the firm. After MSO, the second role shouldn't apply. Once partners have sold their interest in the firm, they shouldn't be part of the management or decision teams—they might share an opinion but should not be in the room when it is time to vote. We also believe that retired partners (after MSO) should no longer be doing partner-level work, so they shouldn't still be filling the role of partner, either.

In summary, by implementing MSO, firms

- have a clearer path to develop leadership. Firms can attract and retain younger talent because they clearly know that they will have a chance to be the senior leaders in the future, and that they will have to turn over the reins as well when their time comes. This helps keep the best and the brightest working in the firm because they recognize that the system is set up to ensure the transition of leadership. Without MSO, younger partners are often motivated to split from the firm once they realize that it will be time for them to retire before the current senior partners are willing to step down.
- can keep a better focus on the firm getting better, faster, and stronger. Senior owners often become resistant to change and complacent as well as conservative regarding investment in the firm.
- create a process to address one of the most difficult conversations young partners can have with the senior partner who most likely hired them and most certainly supported them to become partners as well as mentored them along the way:

that it is time to step down as part of the management team of the firm. MSO facilitates this conversation. The partner is given notice early on about when they will step down (which allows the firm to line up talent and capacity to take over) and younger partners are aware of when they will need to be ready to step up and make sure the firm is positioned to be successful.

- solve a common problem brought on by age. Although the magnitude varies with each individual, as we get older, we generally get more forgetful, our health and recovery from health-related problems is not as robust, our thinking is not as clear, our ability to work the hours required is lessened, and so on. We see too many firms in which senior partners simply are not pulling their weight and haven't for some time. In some cases, even the work these partners do has to covertly be redone by others because of its poor quality. But because those senior partners have a voting percentage or ownership that makes it difficult to impossible to remove from the firm, they cannot be easily dealt with like any other person who is no longer performing.

These are examples of how MSO creates a critical safety net so that the firm can move leaders in key positions out before these age-related issues become too difficult for the firm to survive. Because MSO doesn't prohibit the retiring partner from working for the firm (just forces them out of leadership), those partners who are pulling their weight and have a realistic view of the value of their efforts have no problem staying on and continuing to work for the firm. However, our anecdotal view of this is less than half of the partners are asked to stay, with less than 20 percent staying on with the firm for more than a couple of years. What this says to us is that either MSO forces people to move on to the next stage of their lives or very few senior partners have a realistic view of the value of their work, or both. Whichever it is, in our view, MSO positions the firm for long-term sustainability.

Findings from the surveys we've conducted show that about one-third of the time, partners don't want to retire without the firm sweetening their financial deal. This usually occurs when the senior partner wants to stay because he or she is very happy with his or her deal, but the younger partners are willing to do almost anything to get the senior partner out because that partner stopped pulling his or her weight long ago. In every case we have been involved with, a premium to buy out a partner would *not* have been required if MSO was part of the agreement. Without MSO, firms typically either can't meet the voting threshold or don't have the stomach to terminate senior partners that want to ransack the firm on their way out.

The Importance of Vesting

Vesting can be more critical to succession and sustainability than the benefit amount. With the EWYK model, there is no vesting. It is your book, and you can sell it whenever you want. But with the BAV model, vesting is critically important. We like to see the schedules start at 60 and go to MSO age, which is usually 65, 66, or 67. If MSO is 67, we have no problem setting up full benefits at 65 as long as proper notice is required. We highly recommend that the language dealing with the vesting schedule be written so that the early vesting rights are *only available* with at least 2 years' advance written notice. In other words, if you are 62 years old, early vesting rights start at 60, and you tell your partners you are retiring in 6 months, nothing is owed to you for retirement unless the firm, at its sole discretion, waives the notice requirement. On the other hand, that same 62-year-old can give 2 years' notice at that time, retire at age 64, and receive the vesting schedule benefits for age 64. Way too often, firms are put in terrible positions pertaining to sustainability because multiple owners decided to bail out without adequate notice, forcing high dollar sale-of-ownership benefits while providing the firm little to no time to plan for and accommodate this critical talent loss.

Once two years' notice is being given in the process (not required for MSO because we know the partner is going to sell their ownership at that age), the firm can then mandate a client transition process and accountability to that process.

We are commonly asked why we make such a big deal about vesting. The answer is simple. Most agreements allow partners to vest at far too young an age, and most agreements allow people to vest at a variation of ages based on number of years with the firm as a partner (we recommend 15 years as a partner) and maybe a minimum age. It is not uncommon to find that all the partners within a firm between the ages of 55 and 67 are 100-percent vested. In most cases, they also don't have to give notice; in some cases, the notice required is only 1 year. In many firms, even if notice is required, the penalty for not giving it is insignificant.

It is also common that all the partners in the firm are planning on retiring within a short window of time, regardless of age, because of this situation. For example, within a 6-partner firm, the partner ages were 63, 61, 58, 55, 49, and 45. At first glance, this looked like a reasonable spread of ages that put the firm in a good position with respect to succession management, but when we polled each of the partners, the earliest any of the partners planned to retire was 5 years, and the latest any of them planned to go was 14. So, while the firm had an 18-year spread in age, they only had a 9-year spread in terms of retirement dates. To make matters worse, everyone could leave with their full retirement benefit after age 55.

In another situation, the three senior partners were 65, 61, and 60. These partners founded the firm and were all good personal friends. The 65-year-old partner retired on schedule. Within 6 months, the 61-year-old partner gave notice and left, and within another 6 months, the 60-year-old followed suit. The 61-year-old left because he and the 65-year-old were great friends, and the business wasn't as fun without him, and they wanted to spend time playing together in retirement. The partner who was 60 left because he didn't want to be the one paying off big benefits to his two senior partners and not earning much salary due to the large monthly obligation owed the two retired partners. Needless to say, a firm that was, only a couple of years earlier, probably the top firm in their geographic area was now struggling to survive. Younger partners were spinning off into their own firms because they were not willing to pay the large debt owed the retired partners when clients were dropping like flies, given virtually no transition from the two partners, who only gave a few months' notice.

Sloppy construction and management of the vesting schedule and process is dangerous for the firm and makes succession planning almost impossible. If a firm has 300 partners, then this isn't as critical a factor. But when a firm has 6, 14, or 20 partners, being in a position to replace every partner for the entire 12-year period between the ages of 55 and 67 is financially, developmentally, and managerially difficult to impossible to successfully pull off. That all those partners could leave with full benefits during the period definitely puts a strain on the financial end of things. So, not only do we like to see the vesting schedule start at 60, but we like to see early vesting options similar to those in table 5-1 that follows:

Table 5-1

Age	% of Full Retirement Benefit	Notice Required
60	50%	Two years or nothing
61	60%	Two years or nothing
62	70%	Two years or nothing
63	80%	Two years or nothing
64	90%	Two years or nothing
65	100%	Two years or nothing
66	100%	Two years or nothing
67	100%	No notice required

Remember, if the firm feels there are people to take over and capacity available to do the work, the firm can decide to waive the two-year notice requirement. However, waiving vesting notice does not mean the firm should waive the transition requirement. Without proper transition time, how is the retiring partner going to adequately transition his or her clients? There is more on this in chapter 10 on transition.

If partners think our "nothing" solution is too stiff of a penalty for not giving two years' notice, some firms create another haircut on top of the haircut already established under the vesting schedule. So, if a partner is age 60 and decides to leave in 1 month, then he or she would be entitled under this modification to 50 percent of the calculated full retirement benefit with another 50 percent reduction of that number due to an improper amount of notice. (If a partner needs to leave due to a medical condition or disability, that falls under a different set of rules, which we will cover in chapter 16.)

Our reasoning for being so aggressive about vesting is that we want to try to significantly decrease the motivation for people to leave while still expecting to get paid. Part of the value of bringing in a younger partner is to put someone in place to take over leadership and pay off the older partners, but under a typical vesting schedule, it is not uncommon for the younger partners to abandon ship right before a key senior partner gets ready to retire according to plan. Now, the firm not only loses the leadership it planned to transition to, but the senior partner is also in a position in which he or she might not be able to retire, given the unplanned circumstance. Although a firm can't stop a partner from leaving anytime they want, it absolutely can control how much money the partner takes with them or the debt they leave the firm to pay them when they leave early.

One final point to consider is that our experience is that male partners typically want to stay until their last day of MSO, and female partners commonly want to leave in their late 50s. It is not uncommon for firms with all male partners to have no trouble agreeing to the earliest retirement age, with partial benefits, being 60. On the other hand, when we discuss vesting for the first time with firms with at least one female partner, those schedules often start in the late 50s and either have a significantly smaller reduction for taking that early retirement option or are written to grandfather in those partners to full benefits at a much earlier age.

Your vesting schedule will have a significant influence on how your partners will line up to leave. Partners rarely leave with partial benefits if the haircuts are significant—they wait and line up in an orderly way so they can leave with full benefits. So, if you want the succession plan to have a fighting chance at effectiveness, spend some time working through your vesting schedule. It will drive how the line to leave is ordered.

Actions That Should Negatively Affect Value

There are some very valid reasons for adjusting (downward) the value of a retiring partner's benefit. For example, if a partner doesn't

- adequately transition client relationships,
- work long enough to meet vesting requirements,
- perform at an expected level,
- provide adequate notice before leaving,
- behave ethically,
- serve as an ambassador of the firm, but rather competes with the firm,

then all of these conditions should be covered in your operating policies and should have a negative impact on the retirement benefit amount and payout for the retiring partner. Our surveys show that all the preceding conditions are occurring statistically in at least 10 percent of the retirement situations firms are facing. Although that percentage is low, based on our experience, the only reason it is not significantly higher is because many firms have only retired one or two partners and others are just starting to go through this process for the first time. Don't let the statistics lull you into complacency regarding addressing each of these issues.

Don't hope things will work out, and everyone will want to do the right thing for the firm. Establish policies early on and enforce them. Be proactive and prepare for these occurrences.

More and more firms (currently about three out of four, based on findings from the 2012 PCPS/Succession Institute Succession Planning Survey) have policies wherein competing with the firm after retirement will result in a change in the retirement benefits, but less than half of the firms require that a retired partner's benefit be reduced by his or her taking staff when they leave. Given the importance of finding and retaining quality staff to every firm, why would any firm put their top people at risk without at least some financial consideration should a past owner woo them away, especially while the firm is paying them a retirement benefit for the value they are leaving behind? When owners leave and take clients or staff, they normally take the best of each.

Just as bad, less than half of firms indicate that early retirement would result in an adjustment to a retiring partner's benefits. We not only believe that an effective policy in this area should have a tiered vesting schedule that reduces the retirement benefit for leaving early, but also that the early vesting privileges should only be accessible with a minimum of two years' advance notice. Remember that one of the central reasons for bringing in younger partners is so they can buy out the senior partners when it is time for them to leave. Poor policy design in this area will actually allow the younger partners to leave before the older ones, thereby turning the succession plan upside down. The good news is that there is an easy fix to this as long as you put it in place years before a partner is ready to retire. When you consider some of the major issues introduced here, such as

- competing with the firm after retirement,
- taking staff,
- early retirement,
- egregious misconduct in the community,

- uncollectible accounts receivable or work in process, and
- loss of retiring owner's clients if improperly transitioned or if purchased on a retention policy

our question is simply, Why don't more firms include penalties for these types of behaviors? Based on current survey findings, only 30 percent of firms do. Why isn't this close to 100 percent?

In Conclusion

As you can see, a number of policies need to be put in place, significantly updated, or implemented with greater accountability to better position most firms to seamlessly manage the retirement process and calculate a "fair" benefit based on the entire circumstances of the retiring or departing partner.

Once "fair" retirement benefits have been determined, we can move on for the moment to the next step in building the succession plan—governance, roles, and responsibilities. The reason we mention that this is "for the moment" is because as we set additional stakes in the ground, those new stakes might require us to rethink a decision made about a previous stake. For example, if a firm later establishes premium perks for past owners who want to continue to work for the firm after sale of ownership, then that might require reassessing a previous stake we put in the ground addressing the retirement benefit calculation before we added this perk. In the end, the retirement benefit is about the whole package offered, not just a component or two.

Chapter 6: Describe Governance, Roles, and Responsibilities

Creating Accountability

The EWYK (superstar) and the BAV (operator) models covered in chapter 4 tend to follow different paths when creating operational structure. Regardless of the approach, planning has to be the catalyst to develop any enduring, holistically integrated support infrastructure. With planning comes change, and change without clearly communicated long-range purpose creates unnecessary stress, confusion, and frustration.

We have been conducting retreats for CPA firms for decades. Early in our careers, it was different. Often, three to five years later, we would be asked to return to facilitate follow-up sessions. For most firms, we observed that nothing had really changed. The list of issues and their order of priority had changed very little; the same old "sacred cows" were still points of contention. This baffled us, given the contrast with most of our planning clients, who were corporate clients that invariably experienced significant changes during comparable intervals. We asked ourselves, "Why is real progress in achieving identified strategic initiatives so rare among CPA firms?"

We found ourselves hypothesizing that CPA firm retreats were meant to be more catharsis than catalyst, and that the spirit of many of the firms' strategic objectives were "It would sure be nice if we could…" rather than "This is what we need to accomplish." As we began investigating further, we found that the vast majority of partners were truly committed to achieving their stated strategic direction. Their excuse for their shortfall was always that the day-to-day routine of serving clients seemed to keep getting in the way. As time went on, we paid closer attention to what was happening between retreats. We found some firms made significant progress, but most did not. Our hypothesis changed: We believed that some firms are just better managed, and that management is the critical success factor driving change. But once again, our theory was not supported by the statistics for firm profitability and success.

Then, it dawned on us: There are two distinct enablers that are always discernible when major change is embraced. When the two enablers come together, they create account-ability. The first enabler is the presence of decision-making authority, and the second is the presence of a standard operating procedures (SOP) infrastructure. Without both, the firm is only positioned to ask their people to volunteer to change rather than being able to hold them accountable for change.

This chapter discusses decision-making authority and SOP infrastructure as well as leadership issues that can significantly affect a firm's ability to effectively implement these critical enablers. Although an SOP infrastructure is introduced, the real focus of this chapter is on developing the necessary decision-making authority with supportive leadership that can confidently and efficiently create a better, faster, stronger organiza-tion, ready for succession or whatever the business environment brings.

Enabler One: Decision-Making Authority

Decision-making authority is simple to ascertain. Could the chief executive officer/ managing partner (CEO/MP) or a small executive committee force the acceptance of change through mandate? Commonly, this authority comes in two variations. The first authority is voting control. When we look at our small business clients, they have no trouble implementing plans because one or two partners, with voting control, make the decisions, and everyone else has to either (1) go along or (2) find a new job. On the other hand, with our larger corporate clients, the CEO rarely has voting control, yet implementation is rarely a problem there either. This led us to the second authority variation, which we call *organizational infrastructure*, defined as the following:

> Defined organizational hierarchy, roles, and responsibilities are put in place to distribute the necessary individual authority, powers, and limitations to support attaining operational compliance with strategic direction.

With organizational infrastructure, the CEO/MP's ability to mandate change rests in the *distributed individual authority, powers, and limitations* component of this definition. As you know, midsized and larger for-profit companies are typically organized with both a board of directors (board) and a management team. The board's role is to establish the strategic direction of the operation, along with the policies, processes, and budgets to accomplish that direction. The management team, headed by the CEO/MP, is charged with the implementation of the board's plan within those authorized limits and powers.

The Problem

Normally, when a CPA firm is first formed, voting control is not an issue. This is partially because most are sole proprietors. For instance, well over half of the more than 44,000 CPA firms registered with the AICPA are sole proprietors. Even start-up and small firms having more than one partner typically do not struggle with voting control because, often, more than 50 percent of the firm is owned by one person. Commonly, as the firms grow, more partners are added. At some point when adding additional partners, the equity within the CPA firm becomes so diluted that voting is spread throughout the group with the consequence that one or two people can no longer easily mandate firm strategy, tactics, and accountability towards achieving them. It is at this time that the firm often enters what we call "no man's land" regarding decision-making authority. No man's land is a place where the firm has evolved to the extreme of management by committee, stripping the CEO/MP position of any real individual power, with a culture of partners who believe every issue should require a consensus of the partnership in order for the firm to act or change. This situation commonly occurs by what we call the "pendulum swing phenomenon" in our work. This phenomenon is summarized as follows:

> Because significant change often occurs as a reaction against some perceived injustice or an oppressive, unfair, abused, or highly emotional situation, the solution chosen often takes on the form of a pendulum swing, moving the person or organization from one extreme position to the opposite, as if the momentum of the pendulum would not allow for a solution anywhere in between.

Let's apply this phenomenon to decision-making authority. In most firms we have studied, once the common difficulty of wresting control away from a founding partner or two has been achieved by a previously positioned group of minority owners (who often feel a little abused by the time the battle for ownership is settled), the most commonly selected form of governance by those owners is one that will no longer allow anyone to ever again be in control or have the power over the organization that the founding owner or owners did. They move from a structure of voting control in which they were accountable to one owner to a governance model in which it takes a supermajority of all the owners to hold anyone accountable (or better stated, a structure using consensus management under which people are rarely held accountable).

The Solution

For those firms that enter no-man's land, where there is a vacuum of management and implementation authority, despite the fact that the firm might continue to grow and be profitable, it soon becomes apparent that either (1) a change in governance needs to occur in order to reclaim the necessary accountability the firm once had, or (2) the partners have too disparate points of view about the proper management of the firm, so a split is in order.

Should a split occur, once the ownership of the newly formed firms is determined, there is a strong likelihood that each of those firms, due to having fewer owners in each, will have rebounded back to a voting control structure allowing both to be more successful on their own than they were when operating together as one group. But, in many cases, once a rogue owner or two have been split off from the rest of the group, the remaining partners may choose to regain accountability by adopting organizational infrastructure as their way to manage their operations. Organizational infrastructure creates decision-making authority by defining the powers and limitations of key management positions. Decision-making authority will exist if there is voting control or if organizational infrastructure is established to mimic voting control through defined and formalized roles (that is, the CEO/MP's authority is defined by the position, not by the actual individual's ownership percentage).

Enabler Two: Standard Operating Procedures Foundation

The second enabler, SOP infrastructure, is put in place to raise the minimum standards for performance, generate consistency, and leverage overall firm capabilities. We define *SOP infrastructure* as

> those processes, procedures, systems, and methodologies that create the foundation for the firm's operations and that are built to generate the highest level of performance by the team rather than by individuals.

An organization's SOP manual details most of this, from collection to investment policies, from client acceptance to client firing guidelines, from performance expectations to compensation systems, from client management to client marketing processes, and from staff training to partner development programs. This enabler creates a framework for the organization within which everyone is expected to work.

Here is the anecdotal evidence and exercise we ask our clients to work with to resolve conflict regarding this point. Sit down and list all the companies your firm services that are successfully run by committee or by a weak management team without robust SOP infrastructure. Then, start a new list of those clients you serve that are successfully run by a strong management team, and a visionary board, with SOP infrastructure at its foundation. Every time we have gone through this exercise, although there might be one or two companies listed in the first column, the vast majority—especially the firm's top clients—are in the second.

A firm can embrace SOP infrastructure regardless of size, from a one-person shop to a firm that employs thousands of people. SOP infrastructure is strongest when decision-making authority is robust enough to hold people accountable. In contrast, if there is SOP infrastructure but no decision-making authority, the standard operating procedures will likely have fewer teeth and, therefore, be subject to more voluntary compliance than desired or required.

Enablers and Synergy

Although having either decision-making authority or SOP infrastructure is better for the firm than having neither, a firm's best chance for success lies in having both. The former creates the ability to make efficient course corrections; the latter provides the foundation for consistently high levels of performance.

The following sections provide examples of each of these enablers:

Voting Control Sample Scenario

A sole proprietor (who owns 100 percent of the firm) decides to launch a forensic accounting service and establishes an educational program for one of his top audit managers. The manager objects to his new assignment. The sole proprietor responds by pointing to the door as a viable alternative. In this situation, the owner has control and can make these kinds of demands at will.

Organizational Infrastructure Sample Scenario

The CEO/MP is tasked by the board of directors (or board of partners) to ensure that clients are being well served by the partners assigned to them. The CEO/MP (who owns 15 percent of the firm) decides that one of the senior partners is underserving many of his or her clients and, therefore, decides to shift a number of them to other partners who have both better skills and more time to serve them. The senior partner is given a schedule regarding which clients will be moved to which partners in what timeframe. In this situation, the CEO/MP is granted this authority through organizational infrastructure, which conveys those powers through the firm's strategic plan, polices, processes, and budgets.

SOP Infrastructure Sample Scenario

Given the facts of the preceding examples, the CEO/MP, seeking to align compliance and directives, makes a proposal to the board requesting modifications to the compensation system. This proposed adjustment not only takes into account the reshuffling of client responsibility but outlines the penalties for transitions not made timely (for the senior partner) and for clients lost after transition because of lack of scheduled contact (for the newly assigned partner). Changing the compensation system to immediately align and support the desired behavior requested by management is an example of properly utilizing SOP infrastructure.

The evolution, strengths, and weaknesses of these enablers require additional clarification. For example, voting control and organizational infrastructure have been lumped together as if they were exactly the same, but that is not quite true. On one hand, voting control typically grants more authority than does organizational infrastructure. This can be either good or bad. Voting control can be good, for example, when the controlling owner(s) are both benevolent and visionary and when decisions need to be made quickly, coupled with accountability or when uncomfortable change is required to remain being competitive. On the other hand, as an example, the situation can quickly go bad when those same controlling owners have peaked in the size of firm they are able to build and have become comfortable operating within the status quo or are resistant to change. Another risk with voting control is that there are no natural built-in checks and balances; when a controlling owner goes off the rails, the firm is destined to go with him or her. In organizational infrastructure, when someone in a key position becomes ineffective, someone is simply voted in to replace them. Reflect on the following:

Sample Scenario

Consider a firm run under a dictatorship (control held by a person, maybe two, with similar perspectives). Regardless of whether that dictator is benevolent (leads through influence) or not (manages through command and control), the firm's future potential is directly proportional to the abilities, vision, and philosophies of those controlling owners. Because there is no requirement to operate within a planning framework (such as a vision and goals and objectives) or within a financial framework (such as a budget) and because these owners are not accountable to anyone, they can revise the direction, priorities, and resources of the organization as often as they desire without any need to defend their actions. This tends to create an operating environment in which the owners are rarely challenged by anything outside their own personal desire to minimize their weaknesses or develop their strengths.

So, the good news is that while voting control allows the instant implementation of ideas because no one else but the owner has to sign off, the bad news is that voting control allows the instant implementation of ideas because no one but the owner has to sign off. Let's be clear. We are not telling you that a one- or two-owner firm cannot be incredibly successful, nor are we proposing that a one-owner firm cannot create an SOP infrastructure that would compare well to the best in the country. We are saying that there is no requirement to justify why actions are or are not taken or why best practices are or are not followed. The resulting flexibility can be both the reason for a firm's successes as well as its Achilles heel in its future evolution.

Enablers and Firm Size

As discussed in chapter 4, the attitudes and aptitudes required to grow a firm from nothing to $2 million to $3 million are significantly different than those required to grow a firm to the next level of $10 million or more. As an organization grows, a critical success factor influencing its future is its ability to shift from being a firm driven by the strengths and personalities of various individuals (EWYK) to an organization that is driven by strategy, structure, process, defined expectations, and monitored performance (BAV). The following is a discussion of how enablers operate in various sized firms.

Enablers in Firms of Up to $2 Million to $3 Million

With small firms (with annual revenues below $2 million to $3 million), voting control is the norm. Because these owners like the flexibility of making up the rules as they go, SOP infrastructure is rarely put in place. Interestingly, most small businesses, regardless of the industry, love the flexibility of a "no-rules," "we-are-all-part-of-the-same-team" structure. This philosophy permeates every aspect of the business, from defining sick time and vacation days to performance pay. Apparently, the theory is that by formalizing expectations, you are establishing an acceptable minimum level of performance.

There is a general belief among hunters (entrepreneurs) that once you have set a minimum level of performance, no one will ever make any effort to exceed that level. For example, if the firm announces that its employees have a total of five paid sick days, then they believe that is like telling each employee to take at least five sick days off. By not setting the minimum standard, the hope is to get more out of the firm's average employees. However, what usually ends up happening is that the marginal employees get a free ride on the backs of the young, developing superstars. Consider this common scenario:

Sample Scenario

Assume for a moment that there is no policy regarding sick time or sick pay. Also assume that there has never been a problem in this area. The firm continues to grow and prosper from 2–12 people. In order to meet the ever-expanding workload, employee number 13, Michele, is hired. Michele works well for the first 6 months, but by month 7, she starts calling in sick fairly often on Monday. By the eighth month, Michele is occasionally calling in sick on Friday too. After several counseling sessions and about 6 months of elapsed time, a meeting is called to establish a sick time policy. The need for such a policy becomes especially clear after the management team learns how hard it is to fire someone for excessive sick leave in the absence of a well-defined policy. The firm creates a policy that allows each employee to earn one-half day paid sick leave for every month worked, up to a maximum of 6 days.

Based on this scenario, who won as a result of the lack of a sick policy? Was it the employees who had to continually perform Michele's work while she was absent? Was it the employees who never abused the policy but now are limited to 6 sick days? Was it Michele, who now gets one half-day off for every month worked up to 6 days, plus the 20 days she has already taken? Small business owners too often mistakenly believe that setting clear expectations through an SOP infrastructure places stifling limits and restrictions on their valued employees. Nevertheless, what most frequently happens is that in the absence of clear expectations, marginal employees will continually take advantage of good employees, and the wrong groups are satisfied and burdened, respectively. In the end, the consequences of the "no rules" philosophy commonly create the exact opposite of what was intended.

We believe it is far more important to establish systems that take care of and reward good employees than to squeeze a little extra out of our bad ones. We would take this point a step further and say that we believe it is important to build SOP infrastructure that drives off the marginal employees. So, for a firm this size (sole proprietors to a couple of partners), even though voting control is not an issue, the lack of an SOP infrastructure becomes a bigger and bigger burden as the firm grows.

Enablers in $3 Million to $10 Million Firms

Now, let's take a look at firms in the $3 million to $10 million range. In this size range, you often don't find many of the enablers strong enough to drive the firm, which is why this is a very difficult size firm to manage. As firms surpass a couple million dollars in revenue, new partners are added, and voting control begins to disappear. Few of these firms have visionary and selfless enough controlling partners who are willing to give up some of their power and authority to implement strong organizational infrastructure (tying power and responsibility to roles rather than people, building the right checks and balances in governance, and creating accountability throughout the organization to those roles) before they lose voting control. So, they drift from voting control into no-man's land, where no man or woman has any control. As for the group of minority owners who gain leverage over the previous controlling owners, they are almost never visionary or selfless enough to voluntarily give someone decision-making authority over them (through organizational infrastructure). They just came out of that situation, usually a little beaten up and abused because the controlling owners were likely perceived as a little too dictatorial, greedy, and dismissive when they were in power. Why would these owners voluntarily give what seems to be that same power to anyone else right after they had just freed themselves from it? So, the battle begins.

When we wrote our first book on this topic in 2004, our experience was that by the time a firm grows to about $6 million in revenue, the owners had to find a way to embrace organizational infrastructure (board, managing partner, line-partner roles, responsibilities, expectations, competencies, and so on) or they would likely have to split up into several smaller-sized firms to reestablish order through voting control. However, we have found firms to be incredibly creative and resourceful in their ability to put off change and simply coast along, continuing to do what they have always done. Although they knew their systems were breaking or broken, these firms were comforted by that fact that it was at least a "broken" system to which they had become accustomed. So, in reality, firms commonly drift in this no-man's land between $3 million and $10 million in volume. We have encountered a few who have grown to in excess of $15 million in revenues in the same desert. Often, the firms on the larger end of the spectrum operating this way (or drifting this way) are a little more disguised because they are made up of multiple EWYK offices that operate predominantly on their own performance. We might find a $12-million-dollar firm with three $4 million offices, with each office operating independently under office voting control (or sometimes controlled by book size, which then converts to voting).

Plenty of firms in this size range do realize that it is time to make changes. When these firms step up and embrace organizational and SOP infrastructure, they then give the firm the momentum and accountability to find their way out of drifting in the desert and back into a structure that allows them to run their firm like a business again.

There is a natural cycle that occurs for some firms under which the owners just can't get beyond the EWYK philosophy. The good news is that a few superstars within a firm can, over and over, grow that firm to a point that it moves into no-man's land due to its success. In order to get out of the desert, the firm splits up creating small enough firms to reinstate voting control with the preferred Superstar model fully effective again. Then, because accountability and direction are easily maintained, the firm will enjoy substantial growth again and grow right back into no-man's land.

For firms in this size range to continue to grow, we find they have to embrace organizational infrastructure, or they will simply move back and forth from voting control–EWYK to no man's land–EWYK, then back and forth following the same path again—adding more partners, losing voting control, spinning, and then deciding that the only solution is to split up and start over as a smaller firm. Obviously, not everyone breaks up. A number of firms simply get stuck in this gap and stagnate, with complacent partners just trying to hold on to what they have. Such a firm doesn't make the necessary investment in people, technology, and management, and slowly but surely loses its competitive advantage as the wind in its sails is wasted by the countervailing weight of its anchors. This complacency can remain for quite a while, or even for a long time, until enough younger partners force the issue to be addressed.

Why are strong enablers so rare among firms in this size range? In our experience, the following are likely explanations:

- There are too many partners, which precludes voting control.
- There are too many partners because senior partners wanted to hold on to the managers who were actually doing all the work on their clients. Thus, the senior partners devised a strategy to keep these managers by making them partners but still having them do the same work they did as managers. Because many of these partners are workhorses who do most of the work on the clients they serve by themselves, the average partner has a small book of somewhere between $500,000 and $800,000.
- The firm has evolved through merger, resulting in a firm that is large in terms of gross revenues but really functions as several smaller firms that are only loosely connected. The firm is most likely trying to operate under the Superstar model, and every partner believes that he or she is entitled to steer the sailboat (or drop an anchor whenever he or she chooses).
- With the retirement of one of the partners, the firm lost voting control because the retiree held dictatorial command and control (and probably was a bullying personality). The remaining partners each have fairly equal voting rights, but no one has the control once held by the dictatorial partner. The response of the remaining partners regarding authority will tend to swing 180 degrees in the other direction. The result is a kinder and gentler, but ineffective, "we-are-all-in-this-together" management by consensus approach.

The more partners in a firm, the more it has to rely on both organizational and SOP infrastructure to keep the firm heading toward a preferred destination. Because a firm in this volume group typically lacks an established organizational infrastructure, the CEO/MP rarely has a chance to be as effective as a typical industry CEO. Based on our personal experience, the vast majority of CEO/MPs that do not have voting control and haven't established strong organizational and SOP infrastructure are consensus builders with little to no ability to mandate change. Their job is to keep the firm moving forward by taking the path of least resistance, which is apt to be the path that no one really wants, but no one really hates, either. To make a bad situation worse, typically, no one has the authority to hold people accountable to existing policies regarding management processes, so rules and procedures are applied inconsistently. For example, it is common for each of the tax partners to process tax returns based on their preferences rather than be forced to follow the firm-mandated policies and processes. This then forces each staff person, before they start working on a tax return, to consider which partner he or she is working for in order to determine how to approach the work.

And unfortunately, this is just the tip of the iceberg. For instance, it wouldn't be uncommon for each partner in this structure to be able to override policy by simply asserting, "That is not acceptable to my clients, so I am not going to comply." This situation does not get better with time; it only gets worse. Anytime you have a hierarchy where client desire (which is really partner desire disguised as client desire) trumps firm desire, you have the perfect breeding ground for dysfunction.

Enablers in Firms in Excess of $10 Million Dollars

Most firms larger than $10 million realize that it is necessary to embrace organizational infrastructure if they want to create decision-making hierarchy. There are certainly exceptions to this volume bracketing, but larger firms also tend to grasp the need for holistically integrating SOP infrastructure. As firms move above $20 million in revenue, both organizational and SOP infrastructure are usually at the heart of their operating strategies. However, going back to chapter 4 on models, even firms this size and larger will still commonly have some remnants of the EWYK philosophies creating havoc, contradiction, and confusion within the organization.

This is not to say that firms are wrong, unsuccessful, or headed for failure if they don't adopt an operator model. A given firm may be one of the best in the country as long as a superstar is at the helm. The ideas in this book may resonate more significantly for the same firm when contemplating how the firm will operate when the superstar is no longer there. Here's the real question: When the current senior management team retires, do the partners feel secure about the long-term viability of the firm? If they don't, it is likely that the firm is built around individuals (the Superstar model) rather than process and structure (the Operator model). We are proposing that a natural evolution is observable among successful firms as they grow and prosper, namely, that they mature as follows:

- From the superstar to the operator model
- From voting control to organizational infrastructure
- From "no rules" to an SOP infrastructure

Decision-Making Authority

Voting Control Properties

Voting control is typically manifested by the following:

- One partner owns more than 50 percent of the firm.
- Two partners who own more than 50 percent of the firm and have a long-lived special relationship of trust, have the same basic personal goals for the firm, and rely on each other for perspective.
- Any decision, other than those expressly reserved by the owner agreement as needing a higher threshold of vote than this one- or two-partner voting bloc, can be mandated to everyone in the firm, including hiring and firing partners, setting retirement formulas, buyout formulas, compensation, and process and procedure.

Organization Infrastructure Properties

Organizational infrastructure is typically manifested through the following:[1]

- Creation of a board of directors (or board of partners), which, throughout this book, refers to the role played by this group, not the legal definition of a corporation's board of directors
- Understanding that the role of the board is to establish the firm's vision, create policy, authorize powers, and set limitations as a framework for the CEO/MP to operate
- Understanding that the board does not get involved in the minutia of day-to-day operations, except through the setting and approval of budgets, compensation frameworks, marketing objectives, and training policies
- Structure in which staff reports to management, management reports to executive management, executive management reports to the CEO/MP, and the CEO/MP reports to the board (if there are multiple offices, those office partners-in-charge [PIC] are accountable to the CEO/MP, and the staff in those offices is accountable to the office PIC).
- Accountability of the CEO/MP for the firm meeting its goals and objectives, which is why his or her compensation objectives should be focused on firm accomplishment, not individual accomplishment
- Partners' understanding that they serve on the board in one capacity but also report to the CEO/MP in another. (The distinction is that, as a board, they direct the CEO/MP, but as a board member, the only voice they have is when a majority makes a decision. Board members have no individual voice regarding direction to the CEO/MP, and as individuals, they report to the CEO/MP.)
- Firing the CEO/MP if it is deemed by the board that he or she failed to perform up to defined objective expectations or took actions outside of the powers allowed. However, the board does not have the right to occasionally drop down and take on management responsibilities just because it does not like how the

---

[1] Many of the concepts mentioned can be found in *Boards That Make a Difference: A New Design for Leadership in Nonprofit and Public Organizations* by John Carver (San Francisco: Jossey-Bass, 1997).

CEO/MP is performing. If this violation ever occurs, then all accountability is lost, the CEO/MP becomes a figurehead, and the board takes on the roles of CEO/MP.

Other requirements for clarity of organizational infrastructure include job duties for all key roles in the firm (board, executive committee, CEO/MP, chief operating officer or office manager, department leaders, line partners, and so on), policies and procedures, and having a firm organizational chart that reflects who reports to whom and the operating hierarchy within the organization. Refer to *Securing the Future, Volume 2: Implementing Your Firm's Succession Plan*, chapter 6, for examples of key roles and responsibilities and policies.

SOP Infrastructure Properties

The most basic properties of SOP infrastructure are what we call *administrative policies, accountability policies,* and *processes*. These are practices, processes, and procedures that apply to everyone in the organization and carry the expectation that they will be followed. These policies and processes create the framework for actions.

A word of warning: Do not spend a lot of time trying to draw black and white distinctions among these terms. They are used only to provide a better explanation of what constitutes decision-making authority and SOP infrastructure. For many firms, they all go in the same agreement or policy manual and need to be reviewed and updated on a regular basis.

Administrative Policies

Consider something as routine as client acceptance. An administrative policy focusing this should help address whether a partner can decide to serve a new client on his or her own or must get approval from the CEO/MP. A partner might be limited in any number of ways, including the following:

- Project size (because the organization-wide availability of resources has to be considered for large projects)
- Discount factor (meaning that the estimated earnings of the project should be at least a minimum percentage of the firm's standard rates)
- Competence (to assess whether the work being requested is outside the scope of this partner's personal expertise)

Another example of an administrative policy might be in the handling of accounts receivable. This policy might address when to take the following steps:

- The firm will send out delinquency statements.
- The partner or manager has to follow up personally to collect.
- The firm penalizes the partner for clients that don't pay.
- Future work is stopped because of the delinquency.
- The account is turned over for collection.

These questions may sound trivial or seem to be an exercise in documenting minutia, but an unbelievable number of partners get involved in very serious conflicts over such issues.

> **Sample Scenario**
>
> Consider Steve, a partner with the second largest book of business. One of his good clients has exceeded the collection limits to the point that the policy dictates cutting off current work. Also, consider that Steve takes offense every time anyone tells him how to run his client practice. Without an accounts receivables policy, odds are that no action would be taken until it was too late; that is, until the client declares bankruptcy or goes out of business. In other words, the client would take advantage of the firm for as long as possible in a manner similar to the example given earlier in this chapter regarding the employee abuse of an undefined sick time policy.
>
> In this instance, the partners, in order to avoid confrontation, would probably ignore the delinquency, hoping that the situation will take care of itself. In a firm with a clear accounts receivables policy, a collections issue sees the light of day much earlier, and it is either addressed according to the policy or through an agreement with the CEO/MP, or, if there is conflict between the two, addressed at the board or partner group level about why a partner's situation should be treated as an exception (the existence of the receivables policy makes this a much more difficult pitch to sell).

At this point, the CEO/MP first has to decide whether this situation is a legitimate exception to the policy. No policy should be enforced without this level of scrutiny because policies are guidelines, not laws. For example, what if the account is a seasonal business, and the firm knew from the beginning that it was performing work during the client's down time, with the understanding that payment would be delayed for several months? In this case, the CEO/MP should extend the date to cut off work to conform to the original agreement.

However, assume there are no legitimate excuses for delinquency. The CEO/MP should tell the partner that work cannot be continued until some or all the outstanding balance is collected. Because this condition is based on a known policy rather than just an arbitrary decision by the CEO/MP, Steve is likely to comply rather than resist by tying up firm resources or playing politics. Moreover, even if Steve does decide to play politics over this issue, he has to defend why he thinks his partners should subsidize his bad client practices. This kind of dialogue, grounded by the firm's established policies, is completely different, and more beneficial to the firm, than the veiled threats and ultimatums that commonly result in the absence of policies.

Accountability Policies

Accountability policies can be illustrated by outlining the responsibilities of employees in managing the firm's top clients. For instance, you could put together a policy that requires face-to-face meetings at least three times a year (outside of tax season) for all clients in the firm's top-tier category. This policy might also detail the minimum amount of specific information that must be collected during those visits.

Many accountability policies are incorporated in owner agreements, such as mandatory retirement age, what functions and duties retired partners can continue to perform and what approval is required to authorize them, and under what conditions, if any, early retirement would be allowed. These are all examples of accountability policies.

Processes

Processes are systems put in place by firms to create consistency in performance and relieve superstars of the sole burden of creating and maintaining success. Every firm should want their superstars to perform at the highest level possible, but there is a difference between superstars who are top producers versus superstars who are the main producers. Consider a sports team. When superstars join a team, whether it is Michael Jordan joining the Chicago Bulls, Lebron James joining the Miami Heat, or any of the other hundreds of similar examples, the teams lose, even though the superstars set all kinds of personal records. The team does not begin to win until the gap is closed between the average player and the superstar. That gap is predominately closed by the development of defensive schemes and offensive plays that capitalize on the strengths of the group, creating incentive systems to reward people to focus their talent on how it can best support the team.

Put another way, why is it that certain teams can, with little negative impact, substitute key players with lesser known talent? Once again, this is the result of a support infrastructure that puts people in positions with clear duties and roles that allow them to be valuable almost instantaneously. As the best example from sports, take the New England Patriots. It doesn't seem to matter which superstar is injured, a new talented player rises to the occasion. This can only be done year after year because people fill roles within a system, not the more common model that collapses every time there is a personnel change, in which systems are being built around specific people.

Process can leverage superstars by enabling organizations to maximize the talents of their employees quickly. Consider a firm with one or two partners who are excellent rainmakers. Because these partners successfully go out and socialize, network, and interact with their clients and referral sources to bring in new business, they are called into action whenever the firm is short of work. The rainmaker superstars are expected to drum up new business every time it is necessary—and they do this well. Therefore, the firm grows comfortable with the extraordinary skills of a few people and never develops these areas from an organizational perspective. As we have stated before, the superstar model relies on the natural instincts, capabilities, and sense of urgency of individuals. The operator model sets processes in place to manufacture some of those same characteristics and competencies. The process component of SOP infrastructure is all about creating systems and methodologies that support and augment personnel performance so that the firm can rely on systems that make their people better rather than just rely on your naturally better people.

Avoiding Common Traps

The following are some common traps that should be avoided:

- Firms adopting a new organizational infrastructure, but key individuals failing to change the way they operate. It becomes clear that decisions are more about politics than policy.
- Micromanaging. This is a danger because it is easy. Macro-managing is often avoided because it is very difficult. Focusing on the root causes and trying to ease the chaos in the long term is much more difficult than solving the problem in front of you.

- Boards failing to manage authority and responsibility through budgeting, performance measurement, and policy. Boards need to constantly be reminded to manage these aspects.

- Boards trying to do too much at one time, which results in achieving very little. Picture implementation as being all about the turtle, not the rabbit. Slow, methodical progress consistently applied is far more valuable than quick starts, which are apt to fizzle out and be followed by inactivity.

- Boards being willing to turn over the responsibility of maintaining certain performance levels to the CEO/MP but not the authority that is required for the CEO/MP's success.

In Conclusion

As you decide how your firm will address the various issues raised in this book, you will not all be on the same page. There will be many heated arguments in order for everyone to get to a point where the board has a vision that it is ready to implement. There will be many missteps as people convey more authority than allowed, dive into deeper minutia than appropriate, put themselves before the firm, violate procedures, and shirk their responsibilities. This is all part of an evolution—a "growing up" process in your firm. If you want to reach your final destination, you have to agree to disagree in the boardroom. You have to be willing to share your thoughts without worrying about being judged. You have to be open and honest about what you want and need. Once all of this has been aired, you have to understand two critical success factors:

1. What happens and is said in the boardroom stays in the boardroom.

2. Whatever decisions are made, everyone must agree to support them as if they were his or her own ideas.

If the firm cannot accomplish these two goals, then you will find the firm behaving like Don Quixote: spending too much time tilting at windmills.

Chapter 7: Establish Voting Rights, Decision Making, and Equity Distribution or Redistribution

Voting and Decision Making

To Vote or Not to Vote: That Is the Question

We're not sure that the Bard of Avon would approve of our remake of his famous line from *Hamlet*, but we can tell you that most firms, unfortunately, rarely vote on anything. Usually, they talk about a topic until everyone seems to be in agreement, or if they can't get to that place, the subject is dropped at that meeting, only to come up again and again until the group finally finds a version of the topic they can all sign off on. Rather than vote, they just strive for consensus. Generally, *consensus* means that everyone is on the same page and can live with the solution presented. The dysfunction occurs when topics are such that everyone can't get on the same page or agree to the same solution. So, instead of calling for a vote and determining the solution by majority or supermajority opinion and then moving on with implementation, the problem just sits there, drifting, unattended to... until it gets bad enough for everyone to decide to deal with it.

It should be no surprise, based on our introduction, that we routinely see problems with this approach to decision making.

The problem with consensus decision making is that the "no" vote ends up carrying far more decision-making weight than all of the "yes" votes combined. For example, five partners might be in favor of firing a key employee, but one partner might be opposed. Using consensus decision making, the one person against the idea has wielded more decision-making power than did the five in favor of it, and nothing is done. The theory is that because the group couldn't reach consensus, it would be unfair for the group to make a decision. We've seen many cases like this, with more than adequate justification to take a specific action, that were thwarted by a minority of persons with some vested interest in the outcome. The sad part is that far too often, this minority or self-serving positioning by one or a few ends up carrying the day when consensus decision making is in place.

Another common consensus situation comes into play when you encounter the relentless partner. These partners just keep coming back to the table over and over again, bringing up the same idea or issue, trying to get approval for a pet project or concept. At some point, it is not uncommon for the rest of the partners to give in to the idea just so they don't have to talk about it anymore, or for someone to say, "You know, I'm tired of you bringing up this issue, so we're going to vote on it right now to shut you up." At this point, the vote is being taken as part of a punitive action. Woe to the partner whose idea is brought up for a vote! The vote is not being done in a business-like way or because it's the standard procedure for making decisions. It's simply being done to put someone in their place, and that should never happen.

Also, use of the consensus method of decision making, especially in situations when accountability is not particularly well developed, can result in after-the-fact ambiguity about decisions reached. Poor accountability and poor decision making often go hand in hand in our experience. In any event, decisions supposedly arrived at through the normally informed consensus process are viewed after the fact by some partners as decisions that were never made—at least, they never agreed to it. These are the partners who claim that the decision was not what they'd understood it to be. Or perhaps, if they can't feign ignorance of the issue, they will claim that they really didn't indicate that they were in favor of it. One way or the other, in the end, the decision needs to be revisited as a result.

It's a good idea to strive for consensus as a first pass approach to coming to a decision, particularly on the larger, more important decisions you need to address. If you can achieve true consensus and people really are on board with the decision, then that's great. However, if you reach consensus, then formalize the process and take a vote to clear up any misconceptions that might be out there. If you can't achieve consensus, then the choice is even clearer—it's time to vote. Upon voting, if the votes for the motion meet the threshold for approval, the motion is approved, and the group needs to move on. If the votes don't meet the threshold for approval, the motion fails to pass, and then the group needs to move on, as well. The bottom line is that firms need to learn to deal with issues, debate them, and vote them up or down, and, if appropriate, start implementing them.

Formal or Informal Votes

Some firms claim that they vote informally. Others take formal votes. We believe that formal votes should be mandatory. For one thing, just what is an "informal" vote in your mind or your partner's mind? Do people need to verbally, or by show of hands, indicate if they're for or against a motion? As is the case with consensus decision making, the more ambiguity you throw into the mix, the more confusion and less likelihood of finality and clarity there is regarding the informal voting topics.

When you've finished discussing and all appropriate parties have had a say, then call for the vote. That requires you to clearly state the motion under consideration (and have someone record it in meeting minutes), and then take a formal vote. Count the votes—if they meet the threshold for approval, then the motion passes. If not, it doesn't. It's that simple. We recommend that you consider using something like Robert's Rules of Order so that you conduct your meetings in a consistent manner, and that you document key points of discussion and the results of all votes.

Voting Policy and Process

Consider adopting a decision-making policy similar to the following to beef up your processes:

We all have opinions. We should openly share our opinions. Once we have done so, we should vote. It is acceptable, indeed healthy, to have differences of opinion and strong beliefs about choices the firm should make and solutions it should implement. However, once we vote, regardless of whether your vote aligns with the final decision or not, everyone is bound to support and implement the decision made.

Although most firms are better served to make all the voting public (meaning everyone knows how each partner voted), anyone should be able to call for a private vote on any issue if a partner feels that the group is being bullied or pressured into a position or feels like a more honest vote will occur if a ballot is taken. The firm should be encouraging key behaviors of healthy organizations, which include the following:

1. *Maintaining open communication*

2. *Creating a culture where it is okay, even desirable, to disagree*

3. *Committing to an understanding that when a majority, or whatever voting threshold identified for a specific issue is attained, the firm will have made that decision and begin to move forward*

4. *Once a decision is made, regardless of whether you supported it during the vote, that you support it after the vote*

The purpose of this process is to make sure that the "no" vote in an organization doesn't become more important than the majority "yes" vote. So often, what starts out as benevolent leadership's attempt to be inclusive by building a firm around the idea of consensus eventually morphs into its dysfunctional twin, and now the firm is constantly catering to its weakest link—usually the partner who wants everything to remain the same and wants never to be held accountable.

Types of Votes

Partners tend to vote using either one-person one-vote or by voting their equity ownership interests. Some types of issues can be set up for one-person one-vote decision making. These are typically operational issues. Longer-term, bigger-picture financial issues should be voted on using equity ownership interest, in our opinion. Regardless of the type of vote used, you'll need to identify the appropriate threshold required in order to pass different categories of issues. Will you require a simple majority or a supermajority? Not every vote has to have the same threshold. Some votes need to have a higher threshold; some can do with a lower threshold. These decisions—type of vote and threshold required for approval—need to be made in a way that allows you to create the most honest operating environment. When firms choose to decide everything using one-person one-vote, as soon as a critical issue goes the wrong way in a vote, high equity shareholders are very likely to call for a shareholder meeting to overturn the original vote. We see this as game playing, which is why we suggest critical issues and large financial impact decisions be made based on equity voting in the first place.

Equity Ownership and Why It Matters

Often, the process of distributing the ownership of retiring partners and awarding additional ownership to top leaders is done haphazardly. Then, after a few partners retire, because the voting control was managed carelessly, it is not uncommon for either the weakest people in the firm to have a stranglehold on the firm's decision-making processes, or the ownership to be so diffused or out of balance that the decision-making process is less about maintaining and evolving a well-run firm and more about power groups, voting blocks, politics, and protectionism. Notice that we used the phrase *top leaders* in our opening sentence to this paragraph. It was intentional. A firm needs to have a compensation system that rewards its top performers and pays them well. But the top performers are not, to the surprise of many, always a firm's top leaders. The equity—that is, the ability to influence the direction, values, and culture of the firm— should be allocated to your top leaders, not necessarily your top performers. In many instances, they are one and the same, which is great; but all too often, they are not. This distinction is critical when managing the future survival, continuity, profitability, and success of your firm.

Equity Reallocation

Equity Allocation and Reallocation: What, Why, and How

For many firms, the idea in the beginning is that all the partners are the same, so their ownership should be the same. When the firm starts out with only a shingle, this is a fair premise because the firm is basically starting from scratch, and everyone is at risk in this new venture. Let's start out with a two-partner firm and build from there, walking through the common issues that arise in the area of equity ownership.

The most common approach is for the two partners to split the ownership 50/50. This often works so well because the two people that join together are often brought together because of their complementary skills. For example, one might be very technically competent and the other more marketing savvy. Together they make a great team; one, without the other, is less effective. These partners will often divide up the work, too. One might hate the administrative issues that constantly arise (typically, the one with the marketing savvy), whereas the other hates going out in the evenings to network and socialize (usually the technical guru). This arrangement can work well— both people get to swap out chores they genuinely dislike for more of what they are comfortable with and enjoy doing.

Although 50/50 ownership is common in a two-person firm, we don't think this split is really the best approach; however, we want to at least paint a fair picture of it. We dislike 50/50 ownership because if the partners disagree, the firm is at a stalemate. The only governance that can really take place is maintaining the status quo. We've seen this type of stalemate situation evolve far too many times to count, so we try to avoid this setup like the plague. On the other hand, the common counter argument for a 50/50 split is simple—if both partners don't agree, then maybe the firm really shouldn't be doing it anyway. Furthermore, in a two-partner firm, one partner commonly defers to the other partner for decisions in his or her specialty area or his or her area of firm administrative responsibilities. For example, in a deadlock, if the issue in debate is really about the growth of the firm and attracting clients, then the technical partner will usually defer to the marketing partner. The reverse is true if the issue is about compliance with a technical matter.

Don't underestimate the probability that, just as with marriages, this level of respect and trust can quickly deteriorate. For that reason, we like the idea of one partner owning 51 percent and the other owning 49 percent, allowing the firm to move forward even when there is a harsh disagreement. The firm can easily mitigate the damage to the minority shareholder or partner by implementing standard operating procedures and processes that define how the minority shareholder can withdraw in a way that limits the damage to him or her. For many firm issues, a voting threshold above a majority vote can be set so that it really does take both partners to agree. But for day-to-day operating decisions, you need to establish a voting process that allows the firm to continue despite strong disputes.

We started this discussion with an easy example and decided to build on it. Let's assume that the two partners want to add a third partner. In this situation, it is common, if those two partners have had a good working relationship and the third partner is added early in the growth stages of the firm, for the new partner to be granted one-third of the company. This is especially true if the new partner comes in with an existing book of business comparable to the other two partners' books. However, if the company is long past its initial growth stages and the partner being added has grown up working in the firm, the likelihood is that the newest partner will only receive or have access to a small portion of the equity—often somewhere between 3 percent and 20 percent, with the most common amounts falling in the lower end of this range.

On its face, there is nothing wrong with any of the splits described previously. The real question is always about future performance. If the firm equity was split 50/50 before, one might maintain that the firm could be in a healthier position now with a third partner because there is a way to break a tie between the two founding partners.

Now, here is the bad news. In our experience, having three partners is not 50 percent harder than having two partners, but two to three or more times more difficult. Getting three people to think alike, have similar values, be comfortable operating in the same way, be willing to defer to each other's strengths, and so on, is far more difficult with three partners than with two partners. So, how *do* you hold the three partners accountable to each other? When there are only two partners and they both own about the same amount of the firm, if there is a major dispute, they will each likely take their share of the marbles and go home. With three partners, this situation is far more complicated to deal with, regardless of the range of ownership that is allocated among them. This is so different because the firm, rather than just splitting up into two separate businesses, will likely continue with one fewer partner. Now the firm has to have a process to formally deal with dismissing a partner, a process few people are willing to articulate on the front end, when the prospect of the value of the new relationship is clouding all rational judgment.

To reiterate, the range of equity splits described previously is not the problem; performance is. If the new partner performs on par with the other two partners, getting ownership of one-third of the company upon entry seems fair. But what happens when the new person joining significantly oversold what he or she brought to the table to get their one-third share of ownership? Even more difficult, what happens when the new partner performs so well that their performance eclipses that of one of the founding partners? A common answer to that question is, "This is not a problem. We will deal with this issue in the compensation plan." But we can show you firm after firm in a similar situation (for any number of partners) that has advocated this action and either does not, will not, or cannot address this situation through compensation. Even if the firm can address the situation through compensation, it is just one issue. You cannot overlook the constant damage that a firm experiences when a partner has voting privileges well beyond or well below his or her contribution to the firm's success. For a firm to maneuver, change, and thrive in a dynamic profession and economy, it has to be run by owners who are striving for success, not those hunkering down, locking the doors, and trying to hold change at bay through denial of the current environment.

When you complicate the preceding scenario by adding a fourth, fifth, sixth, and seventh partner, this issue of judging fair performance, fair ownership, fair voting rights, fair value upon retirement, and fair compensation through the years becomes even more critical. If this isn't a bleak enough picture, consider a firm that is very well managed and very profitable. When a senior partner retires and a large block of stock is to be transferred to the remaining partners, the odds of damage are even greater than what we have described previously. Rarely will the founding fathers give up their ability to control the firm while they are still working, whether that is accomplished through the control of equity or through governance structures, such as executive committees. The founding fathers often are permanent members of the executive committee, which is chartered via partner agreement, and the founding partners want it that way so they can continue to run the firm. But when that founding father finally leaves and his or her block of stock is redistributed to other partners, oftentimes, not only does that executive committee structure start to fail, but partners who have been marginal performers can also end up inheriting or gaining disproportionate (to what they bring to the table) access to voting rights that will forever change the firm's future viability and stability.

Now that we have given this topic some context, let's take a more in-depth look at the common pitfalls we find with ownership distribution, issues to avoid in ownership distribution, and finally, processes to help you constantly redistribute equity so that you are holding your partners accountable for taking care of the firm rather than holding it hostage or coasting on their efforts from 20 years ago.

To take the next step, we will continue to use scenarios to drive home various points. Let's say we have a five-partner firm. The ownership and ages are laid out in table 7-1.

Many firms would die for this kind of age split because many firms have partners much closer in age than this 23-year range example.

Referencing the names shown in the table, let's say SP1 wants to retire at the end of this year. If this occurs as it does in many firms, the firm might be scrambling for additional partners. But for the sake of this discussion, let's say that they just added JP3 last year, and they will add another partner, JJP1, immediately after SP1's retirement

Table 7-1

Partner	Equity	Age
Senior Partner 1 (SP1)	35%	65
Senior Partner 2 (SP2)	35%	63
Junior Partner 1 (JP1)	15%	53
Junior Partner 2 (JP2)	10%	48
Junior Partner 3 (JP3)	5%	42

Table 7-2

Partner	Equity	Age
Senior Partner 2 (SP2)	51%	64
Junior Partner 1 (JP1)	22%	54
Junior Partner 2 (JP2)	14%	49
Junior Partner 3 (JP3)	8%	43
Junior Junior Partner 4 (JJP1)	5%	44

with an ownership interest of 5 percent. So, if this occurs without any unusual intervention, the new ownership percentages would look something like table 7-2 a year later.

The retirement of SP1 places total control of the firm, for all practical purposes, in the hands of SP2. This might be good, but it also could be terrible. If SP2 was the more technical partner, then there is a reasonable chance that the emphasis will shift to a strong EWYK firm centered on books of business and personal charge hours. If SP2 was the marketing partner, you can count on JP1 through JJP1 defaulting to worker bee positions on SP2's clients so that SP2 can go out and find more business. Neither of these situations will build a viable organization over the long term.

It is also probable that because SP1 and SP2 started the firm, they will still remember the days when there was no money to pay their salaries, when they weren't sure this venture would even make it, when hiring someone meant that they had to defer their pay for a month or so, and so on. They likely learned early about what they had to do, like it or not, to put food on the table. As long as either SP1 or SP2 is still active in the business, those thoughts will be strong influencers of the way the business is managed. The business may continue to prosper and thrive as SP2 might not only be a benevolent leader, but a visionary one as well.

On the other hand, you always have to look at what the model produces. Because SP2 has total control over the firm, the system is poised for abuse to occur. So don't be surprised if a long-range management philosophy regarding building the firm, investing in process, utilizing better technology, developing people, and so on is nonexistent. SP2 will often focus the firm on maximizing take-home pay during the few years he or she wants to continue to work. Also, just based on our experience, don't expect SP2 to retire like everyone thought—as a matter of fact, you can count on SP2 extending his or her tenure. What we often find is that "absolute power corrupts absolutely."

You might be thinking that your firm has a mandatory retirement clause so this would not be the case for you. Good for you. We believe that everyone should have a mandatory retirement clause. But because of sloppy equity distribution, SP2 might be in a position to change that agreement because of his or her 51 percent equity ownership. As well, because SP2 probably controls that vast majority of the firm's book of business, even if the threshold to change mandatory retirement is above 51 percent, SP2 can put pressure on; that is, bully, the other partners to make the desired accommodations if the rest of the partners ever want to see a voluntary transition of any client relationships to them.

Continuing on, let's say SP2 retires two years later at age 66. Table 7-3 is what we are likely to encounter, assuming once again that yet one more new partner at 5-percent ownership is added.

Table 7-3

Partner	Equity	Age
Junior Partner 1 (JP1)	43%	56
Junior Partner 2 (JP2)	28%	51
Junior Partner 3 (JP3)	15%	45
Junior Junior Partner 1 (JJP1)	9%	46
Junior Junior Partner 2 (JJP2)	5%	39

This stage is usually when the stuff hits the fan in many organizations. JP1 was really someone who is a good technical worker, someone the firm didn't want to lose, so they made him or her a partner just so they would stay with the firm rather than leave and take the firm's clients. Now JP1 is a voting force to be reckoned with. If JP1 is not entrepreneurial or is not someone that will constantly push himself or herself and others to operate outside of their comfort zone, the odds are that the firm will become an "order-taking" firm—one where there is a pervasive attitude that you only do the work clients call and ask you to do and avoid being proactive in trying to find ways to help them. Although this firm will probably be profitable for years, each year it is likely to slip a little more in its profitability unless the partners just continue to crank out more and more work hours to compensate. Likely outcomes in this type of situation include the following:

- Revenues will stagnate or decline because the firm is not actively bringing in more business than will naturally fall out. Through no fault of anyone at the firm, clients will constantly leave because they need additional services not offered, they are retiring or selling their businesses, and so on. There will also be clients who leave due to someone's fault at the firm, such as poor service or lack of demonstrated proactive interest in helping them.

- Because of a flattening of revenues and the lack of proactive service to clients, key people, usually the more senior staff in the firm, will likely perceive that they need to move on to another organization in which opportunities are expanding rather than contracting.

- As key people leave, a greater gap in talent is created between the partners and staff. This forces the partners to work more hours to make the same amount of money.

- Because partners are not proactive about serving clients or not constantly trying to find additional ways to serve them, fees and realization tend to suffer as "order-taker partners" tend to utilize discount pricing for their client retention strategy rather than being willing to charge standard fees and providing value-added services.

- Because the partners are not spending a lot of time developing people (because they are so busy doing the work) and the day-to-day focus is not on building the future capability of the firm, partners start creating silos around their clients, and the firm becomes a bunch of solo practitioners sharing office space.

And the story continues. It rarely ends well. "Order-taker partners" should *never* be put in charge of running a firm or having too much influence over strategy and performance. This is why equity reallocation is so important to the long-term success of an organization.

If the preceding example were like so many of the firms we see, one of the junior partners would be a much better candidate for maintaining some entrepreneurial aspect of this business than the others. Staying with the example, let's say that JP2 shows a great deal of promise, but so does JP3. Rather than allowing all the equity ownership to fall where it may (default to being distributed pro rata), it becomes prudent for SP1 and SP2 to have a plan that provides for the ownership being spread to those people best suited to take the firm to the next level. That is, SP1 and SP2 need to make sure of the following before they retire:

- A system of governance is installed that can last beyond their control.
- The equity split is done in a way that doesn't give "order-taker partners" too much influence in the strategy.
- They create an operating environment that sets performance expectations and holding everyone accountable.
- Voting thresholds are set for operational policies, processes, and procedures at a level where the vocal minority of ownership interests can't run the firm through veto power.
- Control won't fall to any one partner.

We believe that having these difficult discussions today is much better and less painful than the conflict that most likely will come about if you allow the firm to shift power into the hands of partners who

- can't see the firm as more important than themselves.
- constantly protect their own self-interest at the expense of others.
- don't understand that every partner and staff member has to be accountable, and that you can't have accountability unless there is a formal governance structure that will eliminate the "I-am-a-partner-and-will-do-whatever-I-want" performance expectation.
- think that because they are now a partner, they never have to change again or push themselves to learn or work in new ways.
- can't see the importance of investing in their firm and their people to maintain a profitable organization.
- see the creation of an "order-taking firm" as an easy way to finish out their career in a minimally demanding environment.

Determining Equity Allocations

The process we use to help firms determine equity allocations and reallocations considers several factors, including compensation history, partners' ratings of one another's skills and leadership ability, and partners' suggested allocations of equity ownership percentages.

Compensation History

We use compensation history as one of the factors in this process because the amount of compensation earned typically reflects about how well someone has performed under the previous operating model and expectations. However, as with everything else, although you need to review the numbers, you also have to consider the factors that influenced the final pay per partner. For example, consider the portion of pay that is attributable to existing equity ownership. Compensation for the purpose of this analysis may need to be calculated without this component of pay because it is not performance based. Additionally, because ownership percentage is under review here, we're looking at compensation more as a demonstration of how well the partner lived up to the outlined performance metrics at the firm than as an entitlement based on ownership percentages.

Partners' Ratings of One Another

In our opinion, how a partner is viewed by the other partners is a significant factor. When you are deciding who should have more say (or less say, which is just as important), it is critical to consider issues such as whose judgment partners trust, who is pulling the wagon, who consistently acts in the firm's best interest, who is viewed as a current or future leader, and so on. With this in mind, here are some of the areas we typically investigate and obtain feedback on in this phase of the process:

Technical Ability

How strong is this partner technically in his or her area of specialty? If they are the CEO or managing partner, how strong are they in management and leadership skills? For department, unit, or division leaders, you're going to want to know about both their technical skills and their management skills.

Client Service

Does this partner have loyal clients who stay and act as referral sources for yet more clients? What's this partner's client turnover like? Good client service should result in low client turnover, with the firm realizing reasonable revenues from the work performed. It shouldn't take discounts to keep turnover low.

Trusted Business Adviser

Does this partner proactively seek to understand clients' business needs and concerns—not just financial and tax? Can he or she list the top few nonfinancial, nontax, strategic concerns of each of his or her top "A" clients? (See our client classification scheme in chapter 3.)

Delegation

How well does this partner move lower level tasks off his or her plate to allow him or her to work at the highest level? Delegation involves more than "dumping." It requires appropriate setting of expectations, providing sufficient direction and support, and monitoring progress.

Project Management

How well does this partner anticipate projects and schedule, plan, and oversee them through his or her managers? What kind of a job does he or she do in getting work out the door within time frames expected by clients?

People Development

Does this person take an active interest in the development of others by the way he or she delegates work and assigns jobs, or is people development an afterthought that only gets attention when things are slow?

Business Savvy

How much business acumen does this person exhibit? Does he or she consistently sell work at pricing levels that comfortably allows the firm to complete the work within standard rates? Is he or she timely in the way he or she bills and collect the bills? Does he or she minimize write-downs and charge offs?

Marketing Focus

Does this person look for and find opportunities for others in the firm? Is he or she constantly working to build and leverage a network of influential referral sources and continually on the lookout for cross-selling within the firm, as well? Do they initiate, participate, and support practice development activities?

Ability to Lead in the Future

How much personal influence does this person wield? Can he or she attract a following and positively influence others? Does he or she have the integrity required to lead? Will he or she be capable at some point of leading the other partners at this firm?

Partners' Suggested Allocations of Equity

It's wise to identify how the existing partners see the equity ownership being allocated. After all, it is their firm, and they each have a personal financial stake in the outcome of this process. We often find that there is a misalignment between how the partners think ownership should be shared and how they've rated one another. Comparing and contrasting these two sets of suggestions will provide you with some food for thought and potentially lively discussion.

Other Factors

Other considerations that may or may not be included in this analysis depending on the firm make up, culture, and mode of operation might be managed revenue per partner (book of business), realization, and profitability, just to name a few. If, for example, a firm has successfully made it from Success Mode to Continuation Mode (see chapter 4) of operation or is well on its way to completing that transition, then looking at managed revenue per partner in this process is probably not a good idea. This particular metric would not be that relevant to the firm because at this level of firm evolution, in this mode of operation, the firm is already functioning, more or less, as one firm. To focus much at all on book of business in this process could add pressure that would drag the firm back to an EWYK business model. At the same time, if the firm has partners who can manage much larger client books because of their superior management, delegation, and leadership skills, then we certainly would consider this (managed book, that is, rather than generated book) when we evaluate where future equity should be shifted.

We also like to use various tools to confirm our thoughts, ranging from our 360° Succession Institute Performance Assessment™ (SIPA™), and other tools such as DiSC® to better understand the key players in the firm. Our proprietary SIPA™ is based on primary and secondary research into best practices employed by leaders, and it is customized for CPAs in public practice. It helps quantify a partner's strengths as well as improvement needs and provides a prioritizing process to narrow down the focus on those areas of improvement that are most important for the partner and the firm. The DiSC® suite of tools allows partners to increase their self-awareness and understanding of others regarding differences or similarities in each person's motivational needs. The feedback from these instruments helps predict how someone will behave in certain circumstances. By being able to accurately predict these behaviors, a partner will be able to address ways of modifying his or her behavior for more effective interaction with peers, direct reports, and clients. This is not about being "warm and fuzzy." It is about ramping up our interpersonal awareness and skills to be better leaders. People who can lead, develop, train, and supervise others are worth much more than those who can just make themselves faster, better, and stronger.

In Conclusion

In the end, we summarize ratings using complex spreadsheets, content analysis, and other methods. We then talk through everything to see what relative weight should be accorded any of the factors based on the unique circumstances of that organization. Most of the time, relatively more weight is given to the partners' ratings of one another because going forward, if a firm is going to flourish, it needs to be built on a strong foundation of people whom others are willing to follow. The leaders who people want to follow generally are willing to not only talk about the core values of the organization but also live up to them and lead by example on a daily basis.

Equity ownership allocation is a critical success factor if you expect your firm to continue after you leave. For many firms, reallocation of equity ownership is or will be an important part of succession planning. Although it can cause some anxiety for your partner group as you go through the process, it's better to confront the issues now to help ensure that your firm is in good hands after your leave. It's not necessarily easy, but it must be addressed for long-term success. For tools and resources on this process, please refer to chapter 7 of volume 2.

Chapter 8: Define the Managing Partner Role

Defining the Managing Partner's Role

The purpose of this chapter is to review some best practices about how the managing partner is elected, what is expected of them, for what term, and how he or she is protected if removed from that role. The job differs depending on whether it is being filled under the EWYK or BAV models. For example, under the EWYK model, the managing partner is likely the largest equity partner, or if not, then the default would be the administrative partner. As we discussed in chapter 4 with models of operations, and also in chapter 6 regarding governance, because the EWYK model is usually a silo model built around superstars, the managing partner's role is to handle all the activities and tasks that the other partners don't want to do. It is not uncommon in these scenarios that the managing partner earns a stipend to fill that position, and that stipend is not very much (maybe $25,000 to $75,000 a year). Certainly, there are examples of a managing partner under an EWYK model having a higher stipend, but the stipend would typically fall into this range because the EWYK model is about book of business and partners doing their own thing and involves all the partners trying to live within a loose set of rules or policies designed mostly to mitigate risks regarding work quality while following minimum compliance expectations. It is also common for the managing partner in these situations to have the largest or second largest book while being simultaneously expected to do this job. With this in mind, it is perfectly logical that the firm would be treated by a managing partner in this position as just one client among many, and in many cases, because the firm is not a paying client, the firm would have even less priority than the average client. Part of the reason for the firm's low-priority status is because the other partners see the managing partner role as an administrative position to handle nuanced administrative matters that pop up in the normal course of running a firm. It is not uncommon for these organizations to ask questions regarding the managing partner position such as the following:

- Should we just rotate the managing partner job every year or two so that everyone has to take their turn doing it?
- If the managing partner has client work or billable work to do, shouldn't that take priority over this non-chargeable work?

- Isn't the managing partner just the person who manages the administrative functions of the firm?

- If we paid the managing partner to really run the firm, wouldn't that just reduce the amount of money the rest of us will make because we are losing that person's billable hours?

- Wouldn't this kind of change put more pressure on the line partners because they will have to do more client work to make up for the managing partner no longer pulling his or her weight in this area?

- Explain to us (the partners) how we can afford to pay someone to manage the firm, and why we would want to do this in the first place, because we certainly don't need to be managed?

- Can't we just hire someone outside the firm to come in and fill the managing partner position? That way, we don't lose a client service partner.

In other words, under the EWYK model, there is virtually no appreciation of the benefits obtainable through better management and accountability. The perception is to focus on production, and everything will work out fine.

Under the BAV model, the managing partner needs to be in a position to respond to the firm as if it is his or her largest and most important client. This usually requires a reduction in managed book size so that the firm can become the managing partner's key priority. Under the BAV model, the better that people (all people, especially partners) are managed, the greater the profitability and the better run the organization. Clearly, the EWYK and BAV models couldn't be further apart about expectation and importance regarding the role of the managing partner.

So, because there isn't much to the role of managing partner in the EWYK model, we are going to spend most of the rest of this chapter on best practices to consider for the managing partner in the BAV model. First, here is a quick definition of the role of managing partner.

Although you will find much more detail regarding this role in corresponding chapter 8 of *Securing the Future, Volume 2: Implementing Your Firm's Succession Plan*, which outlines implementation considerations, an *elevator description* (that is, a description short enough to be shared in the length of time it takes to ride up a couple of floors while in an elevator) of the managing partner's role would be as follows:

> The *managing partner* is the firm's chief executive officer, responsible for managing the day-to-day operations of the firm.

To clarify this in a little more detail, the managing partner is

- responsible for implementing the strategic plan and firm-wide goals as approved by the board of partners (or board of directors, which we refer to throughout both volumes 1 and 2 of this book interchangeably). He or she will accomplish this by directing the firm's people and resources within the powers, limitations, and responsibilities set forth by the partner group through directives, policies, processes, and budgets approved by the partners.

- accountable only to the full partner group (the board of partners), not individual partners. Therefore, the relationship between the managing partner and any individual partner, when a partner represents himself or herself as being a member of the board of partners, is collegial, not hierarchical. However, as individual line partners, each will report directly to the managing partner (or in a large firm with many partners, to a department head who reports to the managing partner). Know that one of the most essential roles of the managing partner is to, in fact, manage the partners.

- responsible for keeping partners informed of the firm's progress, statistics, and focus areas.

Why the Managing Partner Is the One Charged With Implementation and Accountability

Everyone likes the idea that "I" will hold "me" accountable, but few like the idea of "anyone else" holding "them" accountable. So, once it is decided that accountability is important and someone needs to be responsible for implementation, the discussion quickly shifts to forming a group of people, like an executive committee or a compensation committee, to hold "us" accountable. The reason for this choice is simple. Because we are one of several partners, we have accepted the fact that a group of partners can outvote any one partner. But, that is a long way from accepting the idea that any individual can tell "me"—the partner—what to do or can be in a position to judge how well I am doing it. As well, by adding more people to the evaluation process, it is easier to find a friend or an ally who will be willing to let the partner off the hook or overlook his or her infractions. Accountability is rarely very effective when performed in groups. If we had an aggravating buzzer anytime we heard that performance assessment will be a group evaluation function, we would surely set it off as loud as we could.

An executive committee, a compensation committee, or groups of partners makes a lot of sense to tackle specific functions, so we are not suggesting that it is inappropriate to have groups or committees operate within the firm; just that accountability isn't a good charge for that organizational makeup. Let's consider what might make sense instead. For example, note that a compensation committee, if formed, would normally be a committee of the board of directors. It is not typically a committee that has unique dictatorial authority, although sometimes, for very specific matters, it does. In our opinion, compensation committees should be charged with the following:

- Development of the firm's compensation system philosophy or framework to be approved by the board based on the strategy of the firm
- The review and evaluation of the overall annual performance and any changes in role within the firm for each partner and recommending base pay adjustments for future years to be approved by the board
- Recommendations, if the situation calls for such, for objective metrics and firm-wide incentives as minimum standards for all partners to accomplish so that the firm can accomplish its strategic plan, which are recommended first to the managing partner and then to the board for consideration

Notice that the compensation committee in this description does the heavy lifting for determining base pay. When certain objective categories of compensation are carved out for all partners to achieve, they would have a say in that, too. But this committee should be established to make recommendations to the board for approval or ratification.

What is not clear in the preceding description is the managing partner's role in this process. The general compensation framework guides all partners, but because each partner has strengths and weaknesses, and each partner has different responsibilities and job duties, there needs to be a customizable set of goals assigned to each partner based on leveraging strengths, improving weaknesses, meeting minimum standards of performance across all competencies, and accomplishing those tasks that are uniquely the responsibility of a particular partner.

For this, management by committee—yes, like a compensation committee—is a bad idea. The most significant and success-driving job of the managing partner is to manage the partners. If he or she directs a partner to accomplish something specific or to change a behavior or attitude and there is no material compensation stick to reward achievement or punish failure, then there is virtually no way the managing partner can consistently hold the directed partner accountable. The most common argument posed here is that the managing partner can work through the compensation committee to affect the same outcome. If this works, it does so not because the system is designed to work, but because the specific people on the compensation committee and the managing partner have such respect for each other that they can overcome the dysfunction of the system in place.

The long-term success of a firm requires it to put in place governance systems designed to succeed regardless of who occupies the various roles, rather than to build systems around specific people and relationships, systems that quickly fail when there is a shift in talent or personalities filling those roles. To put this in very clear terms:

> The managing partner needs a compensation stick that he or she alone determines for each partner regarding the specific, individualized goals set out for each partner based on the objectives identified in the strategy plan.

Please recognize the difference between governance rights and privileges and common sense. For example, a managing partner should

- set clear goals for each partner,
- outline the goals at the beginning of the year,
- meet with each partner to discuss those goals, provide a current assessment of accomplishment, and offer guidance about where to focus additional attention to achieve the goals, and
- meet regularly enough to provide the partners with insight about their performance with time to make course corrections so they can achieve those goals, which would be at a minimum quarterly, often every other month, and sometimes even monthly.

The managing partner's job is to help the partner achieve his or her goals, not just sit in judgment of the partner. And a managing partner should never use their power for personal gain instead of what is best for the firm and should never use compensation to manipulate partners to vote a certain way, drive a wedge between certain partners, or fragment the firm into factions.

When a managing partner is not following common sense values and objectives, such as those outlined previously, it does not mean that you should dilute the power of the managing partner's position. Do not turn over the powers a managing partner requires to be effective to a compensation committee just because you have an incompetent, selfish, self-serving, or greedy managing partner. Rather, fire that managing partner and install one who will do the job as outlined.

It is one thing for a compensation committee to evaluate performance regarding objective criteria (that is, those metrics that are approved as part of the overall compensation plan each year). It is just as acceptable for that committee to analyze trends in pay, performance, job duties, and so on, and propose pay range adjustments. But the pendulum swings way too far when a firm positions the compensation committee to assess a partner's individual performance against customized goals, which are often qualitative in nature. It is an inappropriate job of a committee to meet with each partner regularly and assess progress and provide feedback. That function belongs solely to the managing partner, just as it is not the job of the compensation committee to regularly coach partners in behavior and developmental transitions, as that function also belongs to the managing partner.

Because we mentioned the executive committee previously, we feel we should take a moment and discuss that, as well. Way too many medium to smaller firms (firms with less than 20 partners) put executive committees in place. As a firm grows to 20 partners or more, having a governance level between the managing partner and the board of partners makes sense simply because there is no reason to drag 20 people into every conversation above the level of day-to-day management that might require interpretation or tweaking of policies, processes, strategy, or budgets. Unfortunately, an executive committee in a 10-partner firm, or even a 5-partner firm, with many of them requiring the membership of 1 or 2 founding (or senior) partners for as long as they are members of the firm, is common. Generally speaking, these executive committees have been put in place to offset bad practices the firm has put in place over time, such as the following:

- The senior partners admit some partners in order to protect their income streams. In other words, when a manager becomes so involved with a senior partner's book of business that he or she doesn't want to take the chance of losing clients if the manager gets disgruntled and leaves, that senior partner pushes to tie the manager to the firm by making him or her a partner. (Just so you know, most of the time, that new partner will continue doing the manager level work on that senior partner's book and not really be allowed to function as a real partner.)

- The firm gives every partner the same voting rights. So each partner, whether he or she has been with the firm 1 day or 25 years, has one vote when making firm decisions.

- The senior owners want to make sure that no matter how many partners they add, they will always be in control of the decision making (this usually comes from an EWYK mindset and, therefore, partners don't believe that anyone other than someone just like themselves would ever be good enough to carry on the business without them).

- The partners put a managing partner in place who has no power except to handle the firm administrative activities, leaving all the real power in the hands of the executive committee and thereby making sure no one can hold the senior owners accountable.

These are the most common reasons we find executive committees in firms that have less than 20 partners. The arguments against doing this are pretty simple. Don't mess up good governance processes with band-aid approaches. Address the real problems. For example, do away with the one-partner-one-vote mentality and switch to equity ownership voting. Put a real managing partner in place with the appropriate power and responsibilities and allow him or her to hold all the partners accountable to the firm strategies and objectives. Stop making managers into partners if they are not worthy of being a partner. And certainly, make every partner, regardless of why they were admitted as a partner, live up to the full roles and responsibilities of a partner.

Most importantly, senior owners, get over the fact that you started the firm and know more than anyone else. If you really did, you would be far better at grooming your replacements, and you would be building better leaders. If you can't build good enough leaders to replace you, that alone is reason enough for you to step down controlling everything so that maybe someone else can build a firm that can be successful without you.

Executive committees in firms with less than 20 partners are usually put in place to counter earlier bad decisions. If that is the case, fix the real problems so the firm can be successful and scalable long-term. Know this: Executive committees rarely do a good job of holding partners accountable. If the firm wants accountability, some*one* needs to be in a position to do so, from the managing partner all the way down the organizational hierarchy. We will address more on "some*one* down the organizational hierarchy" in the next chapter on building capacity within your firm.

Electing and Dismissing the Managing Partner

Often, firms elect a managing partner with a majority vote, but to dismiss a managing partner within their elected term requires a higher vote, commonly 66 and two-thirds percent of the equity vote. In some larger firms, the people running for managing partner might not be eligible to vote in this process, but in many others, everyone can vote. The reason is simple. The smaller the firm, the more probable removing the candidates being considered for the position puts too much control in the minority ownership of the firm. For example, consider the following six-partner firm scenario:

Partner 1: 30% ownership

Partner 2: 30% ownership

Partner 3: 10% ownership

Partner 4: 10% ownership

Partner 5: 10% ownership

Partner 6: 10% ownership

In this situation, if partners 1 and 2 were being considered for the managing partner position and neither could vote, even if all the partners voted for the same person, a 40-percent minority vote would control who was elected as the managing partner. For that reason, when voting is taking place, we suggest creating a 2-tier hurdle process for a vote to be valid. The first hurdle is that those allowed to vote have to meet the minimum threshold. So, if the threshold to elect a managing partner is a majority vote because the 4 partners voting in our preceding scenario are the only partners eligible to vote (because there is a policy that does not allow those being considered for the position to vote), then with all 4 partners electing the same person, they certainly meet the majority vote threshold and pass the first hurdle because they voted 100 percent for the same person.

The second hurdle that we suggest would invalidate this vote because we believe that for any decision to be made, the actual votes cast have to minimally tally to at least a majority of the total votes of the firm. In this case, all four 10-percent owners only represent 40 percent of the total votes of the firm, so they do not meet this threshold. Therefore, it would be an invalid vote and is why many smaller firms allow everyone to vote—otherwise, they might not ever be able to meet the second threshold.

There are many scenarios in which a 2-tiered voting hurdle becomes a great sanity check, as a firm might achieve a vote of 66 2/3 percent on one level and still be valid because that group also represents a majority of the overall firm equity. But even more important, it creates a check and balance, preventing owners from manipulating the voting process by putting up multiple large equity owners for positions just so a minority interest can control the final results. Yes, we have seen a lot of situations that would make you, the reader, say, "Oh, come on... that doesn't happen!" Trust us: Oh yes, it does!

The Term of the Managing Partner

Next, let's talk about the term of the managing partner. We recommend a five-year term with no limit on how many terms a managing partner can hold. There are a number of reasons for this. The following are several we feel are the most critical to consider:

1. There is a belief in many firms that any partner can step into the role of managing partner and be just as good as the next partner. That is a myth. Although we believe anyone can be a good managing partner, they need to be willing to take on the job and learn to do it well. For some, it will come more naturally, but managing people, managing partners, and implementation are all skills that are required and can be learned. The problem with this belief is that partners think that given their current skills that anyone can be an equally good managing partner; hence the "myth" comment. The fact is that most partners, considering their current skill set, are not

   - suited to lead and motivate people,
   - willing to handle conflict as necessary,
   - comfortable holding people accountable,
   - talented at managing and developing people,
   - good at implementation, or
   - skilled at gaining consensus and support for change

   Just to name a few.

2. The myth above would support the ridiculous idea that a firm should rotate the managing partner job every year or two. If this is a serious recommendation within your organization, it is because the managing partner role is deemed to be one of administration only and is being rotated to equally punish all partners because it is perceived as a necessary burden rather than a function critical to the firm's improvement and future success.

3. Many change initiatives, whether an internal change in the way all the partners manage the tax workflow process, implementation of a new compensation system, or so on, take at least three years to implement. So we think reelecting the managing partner any less than every three years destines the firm to be ineffective in making significant changes.

4. Most people who take on the role of managing partner don't get into a rhythm of doing it well for at least two years. Also, it takes time to shift client load to free up that partner to do the job, and then it takes time for the managing partner to become effective and efficient at doing many of the new tasks assigned to that role.

With all of this in mind, we believe that a five-year term is the right place to start. If someone does a good job, they should certainly be re-electable. When the current managing partner stops doing a good job, elect someone else. Five years is a good length of time because it allows the managing partner to be in the job long enough to learn how to do it well and implement significant changes, but not so long that if that person starts to lose interest in doing the job or stops putting the firm first, you don't have a naturally reoccurring election cycle to easily resolve that problem.

Firing the Managing Partner

The preceding discussion leads firms to the question, "Even if we reelect a managing partner every five years, how do we handle a situation in which the managing partner is either not doing the job he or she has been elected to do or is doing the job too poorly to keep it?" The answer, as we have said several times already in this chapter, is to fire the current managing partner and hire a new one. However, this process is a little more complicated than it first appears. If firms don't address this issue properly, they will likely never get anyone to effectively fill the managing partner role in the first place because they did not address how to make the managing partner whole again if they wanted to step down or if the firm decided to remove them. Without this informa-tion, human nature will normally drive anyone filling that role to protect themselves first (in ways like not being willing to shift their book or not fully committing to the job). Without a firm's full commitment to the managing partner when taking the job, the person filling the managing partner role will likely only partially commit to doing it, holding onto much of his or her old line-partner role just in case he or she need to quickly step back into it and never fully leaving that old job in the first place.

Because of the substantial administrative role and duties of the managing partner and the natural shifting of client service responsibilities to other partners that is required during his or her term, should the managing partner step down, voluntarily or involuntarily, the firm needs to commit upfront to transitioning him or her back to a line-partner position with a workload, client load, and compensation package comparable to that of other line partners of similar seniority or ownership. There are a number of ways to accomplish this, and any variation that achieves this task is good enough. The simplest way to transition a departing managing partner back is to put him or her in a similar compensation position (proportionally adjusted, given changes in the business) as he or she was before the acceptance of the managing partner posi-tion. A firm can also leave the ex-managing partner in a similar pay position as he or she was previously until adjustments to the line-partner workload can be fully implemented to make that person whole.

The simple strategy here is to put the ex-managing partner in a position comparable to where he or she would have been had the managing partner position never been accepted and he or she continued to be a line partner during that interim. When the line partner accepted the managing partner position, he or she took a risk by transitioning from doing work he or she was already performing well to taking on something the firm felt he or she could do that would be more important. So, although the managing partner should not be entitled to a windfall for stepping down, he or she should certainly be made whole when it is time to step down. Once the adjustment is complete, the ex-managing partner should be evaluated and compensated based on his or her contribution, either up or down, just as any other line partner would be.

The Managing Partner Compensation System

The managing partner should have a compensation plan unique to that position focused on carrying out the strategic and tactical objectives of the firm. Although there can be some individual performance goals assessed, the bulk of the managing partner's incentive package and focus should be on overall firm performance. The key here is that you don't want an incentive system for the managing partner that overfocuses on individual goals because the real value of this position is driving firm-wide change. Chapter 15 will dive more comprehensively into partner compensation, so we will defer sharing more details about this topic until then.

In Conclusion

There is great diversity in how the managing partner role is implemented across firms throughout North America. And unfortunately, the most common variation, once a firm has moved beyond voting control, falls far short of what this position is supposed to be. The problem is, in many cases, that while the managing partner role typically moves from strong to weak in the transition from voting control to no-man's land, under voting control, the managing partner commonly oversteps the authority typically given to the position and blends the powers of both the managing partner and the board into a single position. So, why does the pendulum swing to the opposite extreme once voting control is lost or that majority owner retires: to ensure that no one ever has that kind of unchecked power.to abuse governance in that way again.

Having the appropriate power, limitations, and responsibilities in the managing partner role is critical to taking a firm from wherever it is to a much higher level. This chapter gives you a high-level overview of key factors to consider regarding the managing partner position. The corresponding chapter 8 in volume 2 will give you more detailed insight into how to properly implement this role into your firm.

Chapter 9: Build Capacity for Long-Term Sustainability

The Importance of Building Capacity Through Your People

A key, if not *the* key, element of leadership is the development of people. We believe it usually comes down to this principle:

The stronger the individual, the weaker the organization.

It is important to build an organization around strong people, but the problem is that the stronger they are, the less likely the organization will invest in developing additional or back-up talent—they already have exceptional talent in place. Because of the exceptional skill of a few, there are larger and larger gaps in talent between the exception and the next in line. That gap in talent drives even more work to the exception, putting more and more stress on the firm's scarcest resources. Put another way, the better you are, the longer it seems to take for firms like yours to become better, faster, and stronger, because they rely too heavily on a few people like you for everything.

The preceding principle is true for another reason, too. What happens when the exceptions leave? Usually, there is no one even close to ready to replace them, as the firm always turned to them to get the work done, and they were perfectly happy with that "the firm can't work without me" codependent relationship.

A good part (50 percent or more) of the job of any supervisor, manager, or executive should be to help the people they work with get better, faster, and stronger. If the exceptional individual is the only one talented enough to do certain work, and they've achieved some level of indispensability, their organization will likely suffer should a beer truck run over them tomorrow. The organization shouldn't be placed in that position.

The weaker the organization refers to the fact that, if *you* are the only person you can develop, you are of limited value to the organization. Why? Because you have a limited amount of capacity, whether that is 2,400, 2,600, 3,000, or even more hours. When the firm can develop others—build strong people who can do their jobs—it can create an almost unlimited number of available hours through leveraging the talent of others.

Developing Real People-Management Skills

Leadership development is a challenge for many CPAs and CPA firms. There's a commonly held mindset, often characterized by the EWYK philosophy, shared through statements such as, "When I started out, no one held my hand," or "If they are not willing to step up on their own, they don't need to be working here." This attitude typically results in the underdevelopment of too many people in far too many firms. Those firms look outside to find "better people," but they generally find more of the same level of talent and often end up paying way too much for outsiders by buying into their hype about what the outsiders have to offer. We tell our firms all the time: Don't look to someone else to fix your problems. Fix them yourself. Don't look to the marketplace to provide you with trained talent at every level; you will be severely disappointed. Your best talent is sitting in your firm right now, and as soon as you learn how to develop them, you will be surprised at how good they can be (not all of them, but a lot of them—more than you ever thought possible).

There are several factors prevalent among firms struggling with people development.

1. The culture doesn't support doing it any differently.

   Culture—"the way we do things around here"—varies from firm to firm. But often, a company culture is so engrained with the way they have always done things that it is difficult for the owners to get out of their own way long enough for real change to occur.

2. Compensation systems don't support doing it any differently.

   Behavior that gets measured and rewarded gets repeated. Because of the culture, some firms simply don't pay leaders to develop their people. Rather, leaders are recognized for their technical prowess, business development, or other accomplishments. Most firms predominantly pay their people for the production of billable hours, and almost no firm pays their people for the production of additional capacity with capability.

3. Leaders don't know how to do it any better.

   Adults often learn by watching others, absent any better source of information and training. This means that good leadership delegation and development practices—which are few and far between in many organizations—will be mirrored, as will bad or marginal practices. Consequently, because almost all firms start out adopting the EWYK model of operations (which tends to support a sink or swim model of development), and because approximately 40,000 of our professional's 44,000 CPA firms have 10 professionals or less (which means they are most likely still operating within the EWYK model), most CPAs have had limited to no opportunities to learn how to manage and develop people within organizations that are good at doing this. So, the typical development culture has been modeled after bad or marginal practices.

In spite of what some people believe, leadership and management skills (which we refer to generally throughout the rest of this chapter as *leadership*) are learnable behaviors. There is no one gene or set of personality traits required to be an effective leader. Effective leaders possess a skill set that they employ both consistently and flexibly. These skills can be learned, practiced, and applied successfully by anyone willing to try out new behaviors. All it takes is a little time and the desire to learn and improve.

For example, effective delegation and development of people is one leadership skill set that never becomes irrelevant and will always be needed, no matter what position you hold. Indeed, this skill set is foundational to long-term success and sustainability of any organization.

Learning How to Develop People More Quickly

Unless you can effectively delegate to, and develop, your people, you're destined to continually need to look for more experienced people from the outside (which is a dead-end strategy). Partners and managers commonly talk about the need to find better and more experienced people year after year, with the same result: They get another day older and further behind in delivering the necessary capacity to their firms. This results in the partners working more hours each year to make up for their capacity shortage. In our opinion, if a firm is ever going to stand a chance of getting ahead of this capacity shortage, it needs to hire people as interns or entry-level staff and develop them, rather than spending an endless amount of time and money looking for, and trying to acquire, experienced people who can start delivering the moment they walk through the firm's doors. For one thing, experienced people just don't exist in the quantities firms need them. Second, experienced people are not usually nearly as skilled as we hope they are. Don't be surprised when you hire a five-year CPA that has about one good year of experience repeated over five years. Third, experienced people often come at a very high cost given their shortage in the market. Logically, when you pay far more for someone from the outside than you are paying for the same job developed internally, you create either a financial problem in which you have to raise the pay of your internal people (rarely done) or a morale problem when the grapevine disseminates (which it always does) the pay difference between the new hire and the existing employees filling the same job.

Unless you're really lucky (like an experienced CPA just moved into your town), most of the experienced people you will find are available because their previous employers made them available. When a great employee threatens to leave any one of our clients, their employers will do almost anything to keep them, whether that requires letting them work remotely, restructuring the job to meet their desired schedule, and so on. So, when you find an unencumbered, experienced employee that has been living in your city for a long time, just know the odds are that you will be inheriting someone else's problem child.

Returning to delegation: Take a look at the way our profession has historically "developed" its people. Delegation normally ends up either being abdication or micromanaging. Under the abdication approach, people are left alone to sink or swim. If they don't sink, they have a glimmer of hope. This approach uses the extreme of ignoring them and hoping they survive on their own. If that doesn't work, invoking the pendulum swing phenomenon, using the other extreme approach, a partner or manager will commonly resort to micromanagement, giving the person being supervised no room to grow once he or she is deemed unworthy of having something handed off to them through abdication.

Besides these two extremes, very few other options are employed at many firms. Naturally, in these situations, firms will always be looking outside for "experienced" people because they're doing nothing to truly develop their own experienced people. A few may rise to the occasion and stay around, and when they do, they'll repeat this dysfunctional cycle with their new recruits all over again.

To break this cycle, CPAs need to consciously develop their people, using best practice training and development techniques, eschewing the dump-and-run approach of abdication, and more selectively determining how detail-oriented to be with each person for each task the CPA delegates. With proper delegation and training, we believe that a firm can develop a 6- to 10-year person in 3–5 years. Read on for more on how to accomplish this.

Motivating Your People

Part of taking care of your people and helping them get better, faster, and stronger involves understanding what motivates them. Any number of things will motivate people. Clearly, an individual's motivating needs (that is, their personality traits) are going to play a part in this. For example, some people are wired to be more motivated by an opportunity to take off and run with something autonomously. Other people are going to be more motivated by an opportunity to very methodically learn how to do something with a great deal of initial input and assistance from you. Neither of these styles is right or wrong; they are what they are. Both of these styles, as well as all of the others, can equally end up in confident employees with excellent competencies. A leader needs to know his or her people well enough to understand their motivational makeup.

Above and beyond the very important individual personality differences we find from person to person, there also are some general motivational principles every leader would do well to keep in mind.

- First of all, people generally want to receive wages and benefits in line with those of their peers. This is known as *internal and external pay equity*. In other words, based on what I think I know my peers are receiving in this company, is my pay somewhere in line? That's the internal equity issue. Based on what people make in this position within the profession, within the industry where I'm employed, in similar jobs in similar locations, is it in line? So, if firms don't meet the pay equity issue, they have a dissatisfying situation to address right away. If this is ignored, you can bet that it is going to be, at a minimum, a detractor for the firm.

- Another motivator is having a challenging job with the opportunity for advancement. This tends to motivate most people.

- Something else that motivates people is knowing exactly what's expected of them. Don't kid yourself. Firms can't effectively manage and motivate people if they don't set clear expectations for them. Most people want to do a good job— they want to do the right thing. You have to help clarify for them what the right things are. Because none of us read minds very well, supervisors and managers need to be able to lay out expectations for each one of their people with clarity and consistency.

- People want to be held accountable as much as possible to non-subjective measurements. Anybody who's ever listened to us talk or read what we write about compensation systems knows that we recognize the need for qualitative and subjective measurements, but what we're talking about avoiding here is a random, purely discretionary kind of situation: Dom shows up one day, and Bill doesn't like Dom's haircut (just an analogy), so Dom gets less of a bonus because of it. People don't trust totally arbitrary, subjective measures and, therefore, will appreciate quantitative measures when appropriate, as well as some qualitative, subjective measures that make sense with their expectations. For example, consider the sort of measures of success that can be identified to show that your people are properly and regularly supervising, delegating to, and developing their people.

- People are motivated by receiving adequate training. Being able to add to their portfolio of skills is a motivating feature. What are you doing to help them get better, faster, and stronger?
- The same is true with respect to learning on the job—employees want the opportunity for on-the-job training done properly.
- People like to be recognized and rewarded for overachievement. When somebody steps up and goes above and beyond, an "attaboy," "attagirl," "thank you," or some remuneration, from a little spiff to a large bonus depending on what they are doing, is a motivator. Just know that a lot of people use money (incentives and bonuses) as their scorekeeper to reassure them about how well they are doing.
- People like working with high-quality colleagues whom they feel are part of an elite group of talented people. So consider this: If you're keeping around a poor performer, think of what it is doing to motivate, or more accurately, demotivate the rest of the people in your firm.
- Flexible work arrangements are more and more important. Employees appreciate being able to have a little bit of flexibility in terms of when they can come and go. Obviously, while they are still expected to get their jobs done, a little flexibility about when it gets done can go a long way toward creating happy employees.

Culture and People Development

Your culture will have a direct impact on your people development efforts. What's important to your firm versus what are people are getting paid for? Hours, production, business generated, or people development? What do partners get paid to do? All of these factors come together to form the context for what the firm is pursuing and attempting to do. You have to determine what you expect people to do and what their roles and responsibilities are. Then, recognize that you have to walk the talk. For example, what are you communicating when you give somebody an expectation to develop business and then focus performance pay around their production hours? What would any intelligent person do? They are going to see through the lip service you gave about the importance of business development and pay attention to what you are actually telling them is important by following the money.

We believe that you're simply renting behaviors. What behaviors are you presently renting? What behaviors are you paying for versus what behaviors should you be paying for, based on what you need from your leaders, your next tier of leaders, and the rest of your people? It's that simple. It's a matter of thinking through that process and determining what you need to do to get more of the behaviors you desire and less of those you don't want. What you do (culture, which is what you really believe, reflected through you and your employees' actions) will always trump what you say.

Competencies Form the Foundation

It is up to you as a leader to develop your replacements. It's not up to the Human Resources director or department, or some other person, but you, as a leader. People development, done properly, typically involves a system for

- identifying future leaders,
- developing what your organization needs in the way of competencies, not only for leaders but for all the positions,
- identifying gaps in the people's competencies, and
- developing a plan to help them close the gaps.

That plan might include things such as coaching, mentoring, teaching, training, counseling, and appropriate developmental experiences.

Competencies are a series of behaviors or actions that make up part of a job and that usually require some experience to build up or acquire. They're not personality traits or motivational needs, and they generally are pretty easy to observe and measure. Let's use the game of golf as an example. On one hand, knowledge, skills, and abilities are required to be able to play the game. These are entry-level skills that allow you to start playing the game, including the knowledge of how to grip the club, knowing how to stand and address the ball, which clubs to use when, and of course, you'll need some general hand-eye coordination. But these aren't competencies.

Competency descriptions for golf might look something like the ability to

- score less than (you pick 100, 90, 80?) on a routine basis;
- execute different types of shots with some level of skill;
- adapt to different playing conditions, courses, and course conditions so you can play a fast course or slow course with wind or other weather conditions beyond your control; and
- select the right clubs in various conditions, and so on.

You can generate a great cognitive understanding of golf by reading books or watching videos about it, but you're not going to play better golf until you get out and do the work. Competencies come from practice, experience, and skills developed over a period of time. Building up a competency results in specific behaviors that are fairly easy to observe. Generating a cognitive understanding doesn't.

For a CPA firm, there are some broad competency groupings you might want to consider. In table 9-1 we've listed the categories we use in our Succession Institute Competency Framework™ and related 360° assessment tools.

To identify development needs once you have identified the competencies you're trying to develop, you should be able to observe the behaviors and determine if people are employing them or not. By observation, you can watch someone or take a look at

Table 9-1

Vision and Strategy	Judgment and Decision-Making
Job Competence	Ethics and Integrity
Industry Knowledge	Coaching and Mentoring
Communication Skills	Building Teams
Leading Change	Marketing Focus
Execution	Business Savvy
Leadership Image	Most Trusted Business Adviser
Developing a Following	

yourself, and have other people watch you and provide feedback. Am I doing this? For example, in terms of Execution: Do I set clear goals? Do I hold people accountable for goals? Do I follow up and monitor progress? If the answers are yes, then I must have some level of competency in that area. If my answers are no, then that represents a competency gap that needs to be worked on. You can use these observations of competencies and compare your observations against a competency framework that outlines various competencies for different positions in the firm. Using frequent feedback and discussion, you can work with other people to help them understand their developmental needs and coach them to implement plans that can result in improved competencies in those critical areas needing work.

Part of this can be done very easily through 360° assessments in which the person who is being evaluated completes it and his or her bosses, peers, and people that report to him or her also complete it. It should be anonymous and allow you to get a good, quick view from multiple perspectives of how someone is doing. Keep in mind that all feedback is good; it's just that some of it is a little harder to take than others. Employees need to have this kind of open feedback if they are going to have any hope of getting better, faster, and stronger. We need it. Our people need it.

Examples of Some Competency Definitions

To better illustrate what we're discussing here, we have included some examples of competency definitions.

Associate: Job Competence

Demonstrates excellent skill and experience in his or her technical area at the associate level of firm operations.	**General:** Does this person understand general accounting—basic accounting concepts such as double-entry accounting, how processes or transactions are recorded, and so on? Is he or she able to use Microsoft Excel and Word effectively in the technical work assigned to him or her? Is he or she functioning effectively in using the firm's workpaper system and other firm technology platforms? Does he or she effectively use firm standard workpapers and file formats? Does he or she make sure documents, workpapers, and files are all complete and organized for good information flow, numbers tie out, and so on, prior to submitting for review? Does he or she understand the processes, workpapers, and techniques he or she is using on an accounting or tax job, and why? **Audit and Accounting:** Does this person understand the differences between different levels of service (that is, audit, review, and compilation)?

Senior Associate: Most Trusted Business Adviser

Proactively seeks to understand clients' business needs and concerns—not just financial and tax.	Does this person actively seek opportunities, with management's approval, to interact with clients? Does he or she take it on himself or herself to learn about key clients' business, challenges, and opportunities outside the scope of tax and audit work?
Focuses on better understanding the needs of clients.	Does this person ask to attend client meetings with upper management to shadow and learn how to better focus on the needs of clients through these discussions?
Can list the top few, nonfinancial and nontax, strategic concerns of each of his or her top "A" clients.	Does this person ask management for insight into the key issues facing clients with whom he or she is working?

People Development in Three Steps

People development really is a three-step process:

- Identify where each individual is in the pipeline and what level competencies they're expected to have (what position do they hold and into what position are you trying to move them?) What competencies are you looking for from this person based on the position they're filling at this point? What level of competencies are you trying to move them to based on their career development path?
- Assess how well they are presently performing against these expected competencies.
- Develop action plans for training, educating, coaching, and developing them.

To be able to help somebody fully develop their competencies, you need to look at a variety of different methods for building up those competencies. These methods will involve some combination of coaching, mentoring, teaching and training, counseling, and appropriate developmental experiences.

Do not overlook the power of appropriate developmental experiences. For example, in a CPA firm, somebody might need to learn a little bit more about how to prepare or assist clients in preparing financial statements for a construction company using the percentage of completion method of accounting for contract revenue. What sort of client jobs can you assign them in order to help them learn what it takes to calculate the contract schedule and the percentage of completion and report that in the financial statements? This is just one example; there are any number of examples you should be able to identify for each of your people.

Setting People Up for Success Through Clear Expectations

The three preceding steps require follow-up and some proactive work on your part as a leader to make sure your people are moving along, know where they're expected to end up as they progress, understand what kind of progress they are making, and are getting feedback that allows them to see what they need to do to get even better.

That's why it is so important to set clear expectations in the beginning. Clear expectations remove ambiguity. Ambiguity makes it difficult for your people to understand what you want from them, and it makes it difficult for you to judge if they've provided what you wanted. If the people with whom you're working don't have a clear expectation of what it is that you want from them, how can you expect them to be held accountable and do what you want them to do?

If you take a look at figure 9-1, you'll see that the y-axis shows a level of accountability from low to high. The x-axis shows ambiguity from low to high.

In the upper left quadrant, you see a situation with both high accountability and low ambiguity. People know what to do, there's no ambiguity about the expectations, and they do it because there's accountability for it. This is the best possible situation.

The bottom left quadrant shows low accountability and low ambiguity. At this point, it's clear what they *should* do, but not necessarily clear that they're going to do it because there's no accountability for doing so.

Then, in the top right quadrant, there is high accountability, but high ambiguity creates questions on the employee's part like, What am I *supposed* to do? What am I accountable for? How do I know if I'm going to do a good job? What are you expecting from me?

The lower right quadrant is the absolute worst position to be in. To borrow a line from Dirty Harry Callahan, do you feel lucky? Well, do ya? Because if you have high ambiguity and low accountability, who knows what you are going to see happen? You could get lucky. Things might work as they should. More often than not, though, you're going to find that disappointing performance is the result.

Figure 9-1

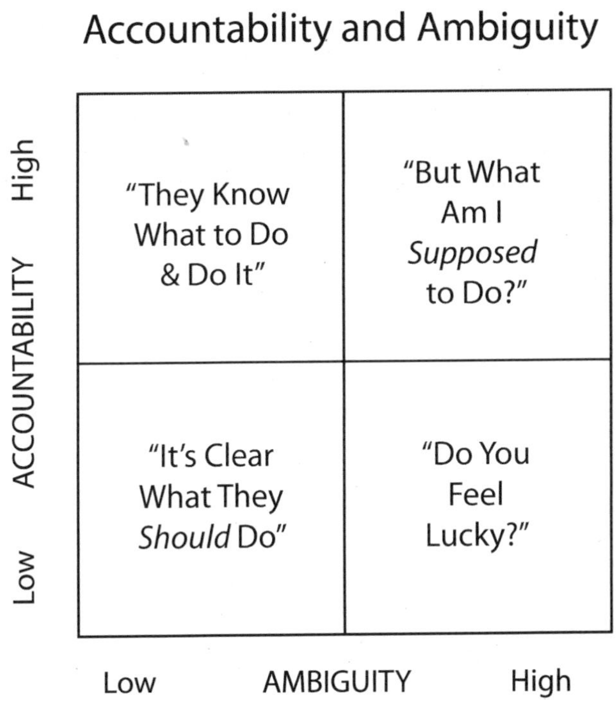

Accountability and Ambiguity

	ACCOUNTABILITY	
High	"They Know What to Do & Do It"	"But What Am I *Supposed* to Do?"
Low	"It's Clear What They *Should* Do"	"Do You Feel Lucky?"
	Low AMBIGUITY High	

Why are we making such a big deal out of the interplay between ambiguity and accountability? Well, think about it this way. Why do people not do what they should be doing? Is it because of the ambiguity you've created by not giving them clear expectations to help them be successful in it, or is it because of lack of training and development, or other experience and skill development, that they need to be successful? Usually, that's what's behind not knowing "how." As we said earlier, most mature adults want to do a good job. They want to do what's right. If they are struggling, it's either because they don't know how or they don't want to. And then, there's the matter of whether or not an employee wants to do a particular task. There are certain aspects of any particular job, no matter how good the job is, that may seem worse to some employees than going to the dentist and not being given Novocain. Therefore, people may resist having to do those little pieces of the job. They just won't want to do it. (Think about problems you may have seen in your firm with respect to getting time entered properly and on a timely basis as an example.)

In other words, is it a skill or motivation issue? In the words of author Robert Mager, "If you held a gun to his head, could he do it?"[1] If you held a gun to the employee's head, could they complete the task? If the answer is "yes," it means it's a motivation issue. If you held a gun to their head and they still couldn't do it, it means it's a skill issue or ambiguity created by you in terms of your handoff—delegation of supervision that needs to be addressed. We can't have good accountability unless we've set clear expectations and minimized ambiguity.

The following are key elements you should include any time you set expectations for someone as you work with them to delegate tasks to them or to improve their skills:

- What is the scope of the work that needs to be done? Recognize that these questions apply to virtually anything you're trying to manage the performance on and applies to virtually anybody you're trying to manage the performance of. Whether it's a partner implementing something at a strategy level for the firm or an intern trying to do a tax return or file some electronic files in your server, it applies across the board. Get rid of the ambiguity by first determining the scope of work that needs to be done. What is it exactly that needs to be done?

- What does the deliverable look like? When it's all finished, what's going to be the result?

- What's the budget? What's the budget in time and dollars, whichever is applicable or both, for the work that is being done? How much time should it take? How many dollars of resources do you have to invest?

- When is it due? When does it absolutely have to be done by?

- What resources are at his or her disposal to help get this done?

- How will we monitor and measure success along the way? How will we determine if we're moving in the right direction and it's working successfully on the way towards a finished deliverable? What metrics will we put in place and how frequently will we check on them to measure success? In other words, we're asking the question: How are we going to know if it's working? It's not simply a matter of input; it's also a matter of output. What results are we seeing along the way to make sure that we're on the right track?

Don't forget about the need to tailor your handoff and oversight for people. Have you ever heard an employee say, "Everybody *micromanages* me around here, and I'm always

---

[1] Robert F. Mager and Peter Pipe, *Analyzing Performance Problems, 3rd Edition* (Atlanta: Center for Effective Performance, 1997).

under somebody's microscope while I'm working for their clients"? Micromanagement and the reverse of that, which we call *macromanagement*, can be good or bad depending on how and when you use them. Sometimes, it's appropriate to pay closer attention to the details of what someone is doing on a more frequent basis. If you come to me and give me a task that I've never done before and that I don't have any idea how to do, I might appreciate some more detailed oversight in terms of your giving me more directions, telling me more of the steps that need to be done, and checking in with me more frequently to make sure that I'm not getting stuck on one of the steps.

On the other hand, if I'm a consummate expert when it comes to doing this particular task, and you try to give me detailed instructions for step 1 through step 20 to get it done and continually check in with me to see how I'm doing, that's going to feel like micromanagement. My attitude is likely going to be, "I'm going to get it done right and on time, so back off."

Anyone in a leadership position needs to really take a close look at how well they are balancing the amount of attention they are paying to a particular person as well as the detail they're providing that same person for the task he or she is performing given his or her experience and past success doing it. It's all about the work you've assigned to them. Less skill and less past success regarding an assignment means you need more detailed oversight (or micromanagement, which, in this case, would simply be proper management). More skill and more past success regarding a particular assignment equals less detailed oversight (or macromanagement, which, in this case, would simply be proper management).

Remember the skill and motivation issue? Less motivation means you're going to need to stay on employees a little closer to make sure that they get it done because it's a pain in the neck for them to do it, and they're going to find excuses to put it off. More motivation means less oversight. Remember, there's no room here for a "one size fits all" approach. You've got to look at everything you are delegating to each separate person and make sure that you treat it appropriately and treat them appropriately. Ensure that you have tailored your handoff in terms of delegation and that you have tailored your oversight in terms of your monitoring to help them be successful, help you be successful, and help them be accountable and do a good job for you.

The Effect of Your Expectations on Others' Performance

The *Pygmalion effect* is a term that social scientists use to explain how your mindset as a leader has a direct bearing on the performance of your people. To that end, consider the musical *My Fair Lady*. It is a story about a young, working-class English girl who is befriended by Dr. Henry Higgins, a professor who, through his coaching and development, moves her from being in a lower social strata to being a "classy" lady in high society. *My Fair Lady* illustrates that we get what we expect when it comes to dealing with our people. If we expect our people to not be capable of doing anything or to never be able to do the work that we want to delegate to them, they will conform to those expectations.

On the other hand, if you expect employees to do well, if you set expectations for them and anticipate that they are going to do well and you *send them the message that they're going to do well*, with the support they need, they will conform to those expectations. Consider also that when you are expecting your people to do well, you are going to look for something that they do well. When they make a mistake, you are likely to think to yourself, "Oh, they are really good at this; we all make mistakes, so it's not a big deal." But when you're expecting someone to perform poorly, you will look for their mistakes, and when they do something good, you likely write that off as them just being lucky. In short, if we are looking for something bad, we will write off the good, and if we're looking for something good, we will write off the bad. It is no wonder our people often turn out exactly like we thought they would—what a bizarre coincidence that we so often find what we are looking for.

Values Matter

As leaders, your biggest contribution is to provide both consistency and flexibility. Consider the following questions when assessing your success in these areas.

First of all, values matter. What are your core values, your guiding principles that explain how we behave in our organization? Have you identified them? Are you living them out on a day-to-day basis? Are they values in action?

Are you "walking the talk" as a leader? Are you setting the tone?

Have you eliminated inconsistencies in your behaviors? Nobody wants to come to work trying to figure out whether Dr. Jekyll or Mr. Hyde showed up in the boss's office today. We need to be consistent because our people need consistency from us.

At the same time, our people need us to be flexible to meet their developmental needs. Sometimes, on certain tasks and activities, your people are going to need more or less direction and oversight. We need to be ready and able to provide the right levels of management to fit a particular situation at a particular point in time.

Reporting Models

Some of you may be wondering just how to pull all of this off. In our experience, many firms encounter problems in developing their people due to the structure and reporting process in place for getting work done.

The following are two different models: a direct reporting model and a staff pool model. It's very common in a CPA firm to have everybody working for or with somebody else throughout whatever assignments and projects they get. Depending on the project, anybody could be working for anybody. That's fine. But when it comes to developing people, we need to have a direct reporting model that says "I have a boss, one boss, who develops me and makes sure that I'm getting better, faster, and stronger." This boss is making sure that I am put on projects that give me the diversity of training that I need. When three people come to me and say, "I need you to do something," and I don't have enough time to do all of them, somebody needs to say, "Do this one, and I will fight the other battles for you."

We can't tell you how often the youngest staff member in a firm has to decide who at the top they are going to irritate. Just look at figure 9-2. There are three partners, two managers, and four staff members. All the staff report to all the managers. All the staff report to all the partners. When one of the managers tells one of the staff to do something, they probably just do it. When two of the managers tell them to do something, it gets a little more complicated. What if two managers and two partners tell them to do something, and they don't have enough time? Everyone has to report to

Figure 9-2

Reporting Models

Direct Reports Model:

—Each staff reports to a manager

—Each manager is responsible for keeping his/her staff busy

Staff Pool Model:

—Everyone works for everyone

Developmental Chaos

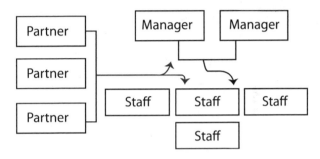

someone so your people don't have to fight those battles. Otherwise, they have an 80 percent or higher probability of irritating somebody every time they pick up something to work on.

There's nothing wrong with utilizing a matrix organization, where depending on the project, you're working for different people, but even when using a matrix organization, the firm needs a hierarchy in which somebody is responsible for developing each person and helping them manage their career.

Once you put in a direct reporting structure to make sure your people are properly and timely developed, don't forget to also put into your compensation model an incentive for those who are doing the developing. Don't worry, we detail this and much more regarding developing capacity in volume 2.

In Conclusion

In the final analysis, your firm may have some great clients. You may be charging something approaching market rates for the work you do. You yourself (and your partners, if applicable) may have a sterling reputation in the marketplace. That is all well and good. Without good people, and your ability to constantly generate additional quality capacity when you need it, your practice will be limited, its overall value will be minimal, and your exit strategy will be weak.

People development, as with any other endeavor of value, will take some time. If you have several years to go between now and your intended retirement date, think about how you might reconfigure the way you spend your time to better address the need for people development. You owe it to your people and yourself. It may take time, but the good news is there is probably nothing you could do that would give both groups a better payoff. Volume 2 will guide you through the steps you need to take to get there.

Chapter 10: Transition Client and Referral Relationships

Why You Need Solid Transitioning

We find that the transitioning process—when a partner on his or her way out begins to step away and get others more involved in client and referral relationships—is the single most abused part of the succession process. The reason for this is that both sides, the partner nearing the date of retirement (often, that trigger is the date of mandatory sale of ownership [MSO], or sometimes it is simply a partner deciding it is time to retire) and the remaining partners, are motivated to do the wrong things. For example, it is in the best interest of retiring partners to not transition their clients because if they don't, the firm will need to cut an additional financial deal with them to keep the retiring partner around to continue to work on or transition the clients they should have transitioned before retirement. If this isn't bad enough, the retired partners inappropriately have a great deal of leverage because they are now entitled to their full retirement pay and still have control over some or most of their client base. This allows the retired partners to continually demand additional perks and benefits from the partner group by basically holding those non-transitioned clients hostage (that is, reselling the clients they should have transitioned but didn't to the firm again). Unfortunately, this situation seems to be more the norm than the exception.

It doesn't take a genius to determine that it is not prudent to buy a client group more than once from the same person. CPAs are really smart—how can this happen so often? This brings us to the dysfunction on the other side of the transaction. As a partner is nearing retirement or MSO, the remaining partners want to keep their income up and their workload down. The best way to keep the income of the remaining partners up is for the retiring partners to keep doing the work they are already doing. Maybe the retiring partner will be asked to make an introduction here or there as part of their transition duties, but they are also expected to keep doing the work (which basically means continuing to interact with the clients and put in charge hours doing the client work). This is exactly the opposite of what the transition process should be about. Transition is a deliberate process to move the retiring partner and the client away from each other while putting someone else in between them so that a new relationship can be formed. The transition should occur over a period of time, so even though the client knows a new partner or person is now responsible for their account, their friend—the retiring partner—is still around in case a big problem emerges.

A clear barrier to the remaining partners taking the right steps for effective transitioning is that the remaining partners often simply don't want to pay for someone to transition clients and referral sources—they just want to pay for work being performed. Our experience shows that this is an economically poor choice. When you have a partner two years from MSO, or an earlier retirement date if so chosen, the best things they can be doing with their time include the following:

- Taking on more technical work in the background
- Spending time working their client transition plan
- Introducing others to their personal networks
- Using their skills and reputation to sell new business
- Training others in their area of expertise
- Acting as an ambassador for the firm
- Serving on local boards of directors
- Other related activities

So, the retiring partner is motivated to keep the relationships (both client and referral) to gain greater benefits for themselves, and the remaining partners are motivated to let retiring partners do what they have always done because the remaining partners don't want to personally take on the extra workload a minute before it is required, and do want the retiring partner to be fully productive until the day he or she leaves.

Benefits of Proper Transitioning

The concern of the remaining partners is commonly, "If they just take on the transition-related responsibilities we just described, the retiring partners won't be able to earn the pay they are getting, at least given our current compensation formula. The retiring partners don't want to take a pay cut, and we don't want to pay them for just sitting around." Our first recommendation to the remaining partners is, bluntly, get over it. Yes, it is probable that in their last two years as active partners, the transitioning partners will be overpaid by at least a little based on the current active line-partner compensation plan. But if the firm doesn't have the retiring partners begin to focus on the roles that are appropriate for post-retirement status now, it can rest assured that they won't have an easy transition to those roles after retirement. If the retiring partners don't make the transition and find a way to be valuable to the firm during those last two years, then that should end the discussion about whether the partner group should be open to retaining retired partners in some reduced capacity after retirement. The benefit of being able to draw this critical line is worth far more money than any amount the remaining partners might pay (or believe that they might be overpaying) the transitioning partners during those last two years.

This isn't even the best benefit, financially or otherwise, to the firm during this transition period. During this two-year period, the retiring partner will follow a specific action plan to take a backseat to the person taking over the client account. This gives the new partner the time needed to build a strong relationship with their new clients. By doing this, not only is the cash flow value from those transitioned clients retained by the firm when the partner retires, but this process keeps that retired partner from holding the firm hostage for additional perks post-retirement. Trust us: Any overpayment you feel you are making to the partners during this transition period will be far less than the ransoms we commonly see demanded from the retired partners and paid by the remaining partners that come in the form of office space, support staff, post-retirement base salaries, bonuses, travel, continued leadership roles, and so much more. As well, once the firm accepts and realizes the need to pay typically earned compensation to the transitioning partners for doing other than normal line-partner work, firms become very creative in finding new ways and specific focus areas that allow these talented people to deliver value.

Understand that the best money you will spend as remaining partners is to make sure the retiring partners do what is most important for the firm, which is to turn over their clients and referral sources, and take a step back in their visibility to those relationships. During this same timeframe, this transition period lets you test and see what other kinds of roles each retiring partner might fill to support the future success of your firm in a non-client management, non-leadership capacity. If the retiring partner can't make the changes required during this period, then that tells everyone that when retirement does occur, that will be the retiring partner's last day of work. If you don't proactively take charge of this transition process and force the retiring partners to move into a transition phase, then based on our experience, they won't. Although you will most likely make a little more money during the final two transition years by not forcing the issue, you will almost certainly lose many multiples of that amount in the following years.

A Transitioning Process

The simplest way to describe the phase-out process is that the retiring owner has to become "systematically incompetent." This is very hard for people that pride themselves on their technical prowess. Here's how it works: Throughout the transition period, the retiring owner

- needs to understand that he or she should constantly be selling the competence of the person replacing him or her.
- should be, with each passing month, less and less involved in the management or oversight of the client work and should be purposely demonstrating to the client that he or she is unaware of project status or outstanding issues.
- stops answering business-related questions during nonbusiness hours or during personal activities with the client. (If this does occur, the retiring owner will undermine the person taking over the account.) The retiring owner needs to reply with statements like, "Let me get back to you. I want to run this by Sue since she is more up to date on your situation. One of us will get back to you tomorrow morning." This shows that the retiring owner still cares, but that the current client-service manager is thought of as an essential resource to providing quality service.

It's very important that these steps are followed consistently and continually, or all of your hard work will be for naught. For example, a client transition could be going very smoothly, and then, a year into the process, the client calls the owner at home for help, and he or she responds instantly with a solution instead of referring the client to the new contact at the firm. In that moment, the retiring owner will have undermined a year's worth of effort by making it clear to the client that he or she is still the go-to person. If trapped by a client who insists on seeking advice or information from the retiring owner, the retiring owner should sell the skills of the new partner in charge of the client while admitting that they don't want to answer because they have not been staying as current as they used to.

With this in mind, let's review the transition process we recommend. We break it down into a few simple steps:

- A transition plan is created for each retiring partner two years from the date of retirement or MSO (if your firm is transitioning clients or client groups who each generate $300,000 or more per year, a three-year transition would be appropriate for those clients, unless they already know and are comfortable with the partner who will be taking over the account management responsibility).

- The managing partner is the one person responsible for creating the plan, which outlines every client the retiring partner manages (if it is the managing partner who is retiring, then a new managing partner should be identified, and that person should be managing this plan as well as actively taking on the role of the managing partner position during this period).

- "A"-level clients will be the first to be transitioned. This is because larger— "A"—clients take more time to transition, typically need to be transitioned in an incremental manner, and are more important to the firm as far as retention is concerned. (See *Securing the Future, Volume 2: Implementing Your Firm's Succession Plan*, chapter 3, for a discussion on client classification.)

- The managing partner should assign a new partner or manager to take over each client relationship. Although the retiring partner's input is important in determining who might be a good fit for the client, it is only that—input. It is the firm's call regarding how to divide up the client base. It is the managing partner's job to put together a plan for this to occur.

- For each account, an action plan should be identified outlining the details of the turnover process. Those actions should be identified in chronological order, noting the timing and specifics for each contact, messages to be conveyed, and specific actions the retiring partner should or should not take.

- Standard operating procedures (SOP) should be established that outline allowable follow-up and involvement from retiring partners once transition begins. For example, if a client calls the retiring partner at home to talk over an issue, even though the retiring partner may be the firm's preeminent source for that advice, the retiring partner will be instructed to tell the client that the newly assigned partner is the best person to talk about that topic; thus, the retiring partner will facilitate that this connection occurs in the near term. In other words, under this SOP, it is clear how the retiring partner will become "systematically incompetent" from a client-facing interaction perspective as the transition plan progresses. (Otherwise, why would the client ever accept the transition to the new partner?)

- The transition plan for a retiring partner, once created, should be reviewed by the executive committee or the board for specific concerns or areas of special focus that might have been missed.

- The retiring partner is updated by the managing partner, on a six-month basis at minimum (quarterly is even better) about how each client or client group transition is perceived as progressing, what steps need to be remedied, and specific actions that need to be taken in the near term to allow each client or referral source to be considered properly transitioned.

Penalties for Not Transitioning

If the retiring partner follows the plan outlined by the managing partner (in other words, the specific action plan outlined in the transition plan was executed), then those clients for whom the plan was executed will be considered as having been properly transitioned. Regardless of whether those clients stay with or leave the firm, the retiring partner is not at risk because the retiring partner did the job that was asked of him or her: transition the client relationship. If the firm still loses that client, then it is the firm's fault, not the retiring partner's fault. If a client that was deemed to have been properly transitioned leaves the firm after the partner's retirement, then the blame for that loss is carried by the firm, and more specifically, by the newly assigned partner. In this case, the new partner had time to build a relationship but failed to do so (by the way, if this happens often, then that is a clear indication that the firm has a problem with the newly assigned partner, which needs to be addressed right away).

However, for those clients that were not properly transitioned (and this decision is at the sole discretion of the firm, not the retiring partner), then the retiring partner is at risk. For all clients that were deemed to be improperly transitioned and leave the firm, one year's annual fees for each lost, improperly transitioned client will be deducted from the outstanding retirement benefit owed the partner. Some firms use a two-year window for this, but more firms are beginning to use the retirement payout timeframe. In the latter case, any clients lost during the time period that the partner is being paid out will reduce the retiring partner's payout.

In the template from our standard operating policies dealing with transition (note that we recommend that a firm always consult its attorney before using such a policy because we are communicating best business practices, not legal advice, through these samples), we outline the following steps to determine the penalty for lost clients who are improperly transitioned:

1. For improperly transitioned clients lost during the retirement payout period beginning on the date of the retiring partner's retirement, the previous two calendar years' fees collected (starting with the year of retirement) for each client lost will be calculated and averaged.

2. The average annual fees for each client lost due to improper transition will be deducted from the partner's retirement benefit.

3. At the onset of the transition plan, the managing partner will assign a value to the referral sources or other key relationships based on past experience. The total value assigned to the clients and referral sources cannot exceed the partner's retirement benefit. Inappropriate transition or disruption of a referral source or other key firm relationship will result in a reduction of value coincident with the value assigned.

4. The remaining retirement benefit will be recalculated based on the remaining term of the payout period to determine the revised monthly retirement benefit payment.

5. If the managing partner determines that the retiring partner is deliberately attempting to run off clients in advance of retirement to avoid a post-retirement transitioning penalty, these clients will be subject to the terms of this provision as if they were lost due to improper transition post-retirement.

Because the penalty reduction in the retirement benefit is about lost clients after retirement, we had to include the fifth clause because we occasionally found partners running off some key clients that they thought might leave anyway during their final transition years to remove them from the lost client penalty calculation. Never underestimate what a retiring partner might do in order to shore up the value of their retirement benefit.

Referral Sources

As noted in the preceding penalties description, referral sources are also included in this transition plan process, with a value assigned to those referral sources. As well, there is a caveat that the total value of the client fees and assigned value for the referral sources can't be more than the retiring partner's calculated retirement benefit. But because we suggest averaging client fees over two years, and because important referral sources usually make up a short list, this usually leaves plenty of room to provide a value for referral sources. One of the objections we hear from retiring partners with respect to referral sources is that it's impossible to assess the value of a referral source, and they don't want to be held accountable for something that qualitative or judgmental. Our response is that, if the retiring partner simply carries out the transition process per the plan, why should this matter? If they follow the plan (and the retiring partner will only be held to what is written in the plan) and accomplish the steps identified, they won't get penalized for a referral source leaving anyway. The key here is that referral sources need to be transitioned just like clients, and if improperly done, there should be some financial retribution for failing to transition valuable assets of the firm.

Sample Transitioning Plans

The key to the transitioning process is the detailed action plan that the retiring partner needs to follow for each client in the plan. For a small tax client, the directive could be as simple as a one-year transition to take over the account. For example, the action plan for a small tax client or a group of small tax clients being assigned to the same account manager might look something like the following:

- Get on the phone and introduce Sarah, the new account manager, when the tax return information comes in.
- Have Sarah conduct the tax return interview.
- Allow Sarah to manage the entire tax return preparation process.
- When the client comes in to pick up the tax return, have the client meet with Sarah to review it.
- During that meeting, pop in for no more than five minutes. Mention that you are happy to see the client and comment about how excited you are that you were able to get them assigned to Sarah, whom you believe is one of the most talented people in the firm.

As you can see, this action plan is simply about getting out of the way and being supportive of the change being made. It only covers about a two-month period in the entire two-year transition plan, which is all that is likely needed for smaller clients. On the other hand, for larger clients, the transition process might take the full two years to execute and need to be broken down into shorter periods, such as every six months or quarterly. For example, consider a larger client that the firm does planning and consulting for. An action plan for the first six months of the transition period might resemble the following:

- Take Jim along and introduce him to the client as the partner taking over their account in either a breakfast or lunch meeting within the first 30 days of the two-year transition process.
- Set it up so that Jim has a reason to interact with the client as part of the preparation process for this year's upcoming executive retreat.
- Jim should be there to observe the entire two-day retreat facilitation.
- Identify and coach Jim in advance on leading some part of the facilitation process during the retreat so the client can see Jim in action and get comfortable with his participation.
- Have Jim follow up with the client on his own within three weeks after the retreat to go over the notes taken, actions identified, and assignments made.

In this situation, within the first six months, while the retiring partner is still in control of the engagement, the actions are all about allowing the client to become comfortable with the skills and involvement of the new partner.

In volume 2, chapter 10, you can review a sample document created for this process: our Transition Form.

One commonly asked question is, "What if someone had met all the transitioning requirements for almost all the quarters, and then for the last quarter or two, the managing partner shows that he or she no longer is meeting the requirements? It seems like the managing partner has too much power over this situation." For the record, if someone has been noted as meeting all or most of the transitioning requirements at the front end and not meeting them at the back end of the process, either one of two bad things has happened: The managing partner has become totally unethical in his or her evaluation (which we have never seen, but which would likely be overruled by the partner group were it to happen); or, more likely, the retiring partner took actions with his or her clients in an attempt to reverse the transition process. Consider a real life example we saw in which the retiring partner, in his last few months of the transition period (because he was frustrated by the firm's unwillingness to provide him with some excessive perks he believed he deserved), told all of his clients that they should move to a different firm because his remaining partners were idiots and did not know what they were doing. Yes, that's hard to imagine, but it happened.

Transition Compensation Plan

In addition to the potential penalties for inadequate transitioning, we recommend that retiring partners be placed under a separate pay plan that rewards them for transitioning clients and performing activities that are more appropriate for soon-to-be-retiring partners. Keep in mind a principle we state several times throughout this book—people do what they get paid to do. They follow the money. If you continue to pay a retiring partner for all the normal metrics, which don't include transitioning activities, you're creating a big problem for the partner and the firm. Make it easier on all concerned and devote part of the pay of the retiring partner to the transitioning process. If, for example, you have between 15 percent and 30 percent or more set aside for incentives, then devote that incentive pay to transitioning clients and referral sources as well as other identified appropriate activities for a partner in this slow-down stage.

In Conclusion

Because the retiring partners have so much to lose if they do not transition their clients and referral sources properly (one year's annual fee deducted from their retirement benefit potentially anytime during the benefit payout period plus some portion of their current pay during the transition period) and so much to gain by simply following the process (regardless of whether the clients leave, their benefit is protected), our experience is that they will follow the plan. However, the managing partner has a critical role to fill, as well. If the managing partner does not identify the action steps for each client in advance, does not monitor whether the retiring partner fulfilled those expectations, and does not meet with the retiring partner on some consistent basis to provide feedback about progress (either quarterly or semiannually for the final two years), as well as whether each client or client group is being classified as properly or improperly transitioned at that time, then this process won't work. This is about two -way accountability for both the managing partner and the retiring partner.

If you follow this process, then you will find one of two things: First, if it flows smoothly, then you will be preventing the single most commonly violated process in succession management (which is proper client and referral source transitioning). Second, if the process is being ignored, you will find out much earlier that the retiring partner is not going to properly transition his or her clients and you can start taking action to salvage whatever relationships you can. Even if you can't salvage those clients, you will at least ease the financial burden of the retiring partner's retirement benefit.

Chapter 11: Describe the Admission to Ownership and Development Process

Who Should Become Owners in Your Firm?

With all the focus in this book on succession management and handing off the business to the next generation, we probably ought to take a moment or two here to discuss the identification of potential owners and your ownership admission process. When should you *not* make someone an owner? In our opinion, if the person clearly doesn't embrace the firm's core values, or if he or she is unproven in terms of core values, technical ability, client service ability, or the ability to work within your standard operating procedures, the firm shouldn't be making him or her a partner—especially not just for the sake of keeping him or her around.

All too often, though, we see owners who were allowed to become partners because the existing partners were afraid to lose them, not because they were thought of as a future leader of the firm. Behind this poor decision-making process is a manager who is the technical workhorse on many of a specific partner's clients. Even though the manager is likely to have some severe shortcomings when it comes to the competencies required to be a partner, it becomes in the best personal interest of that specific partner to lobby to promote the manager to partner to make the partner's life easier as well as to shore up his or her retirement value through greater client retention. This allows the partner to avoid making the hard decisions and having difficult conversations with the manager about whether he or she is truly up to the task of ownership. .In other words, the partner allows the perspective of "what is best for me" to trump "what is best for the firm." Due to partners' neglect of their responsibilities, many firms end up with career managers, who never proved themselves partner material to begin with, being admitted to partnership anyway. We can't think of a worse reason for promotion or a worse outcome for the firm.

A majority of multi-owner firms struggle with when, and if, to let someone into the inner sanctum. Over the last several years, in the succession management surveys we've conducted with the AICPA's PCPS section, we've found that over two-thirds of multi-owner firms don't have formal written requirements for admission to ownership.

Rather, they have informal frameworks that change based on the perspectives of the current owners. This is a "we'll know it when we see it" approach. Less than one-third have identified and documented minimum subjective qualities that someone must demonstrate in order to be considered for ownership. Very few firms of any size have clearly articulated the competencies expected for partnership admission, and the smaller the firm, the less likely it is to have identified anything stable or any concrete criteria on which the firm or partner candidates can rely to determine if someone is ready to be admitted to ownership.

Regarding who should be able to become owners, we believe that prospective partners should be professionals who are capable of being groomed to manage larger books of business than they've probably been accustomed to seeing in the past. They should have the desire to work on developing the people within the firm, together with the ability to function effectively within the firm's institutionalized standard operating procedures and the firm's approach to marketing and business development. They don't need to be rainmakers—they need to be people developers who want to understand their clients' needs, concerns, opportunities, and challenges. They also need to be of high moral character. Don't do business with people you can't or don't trust.

Career Paths for Prospective Owners

You need to leave your firm in better condition than when you joined or started it. This means that you need to be developing your partners to help them become better than you. This often creates a huge shift in cultures, from "How can I build my client base?" to "How can I build a firm of competent, energized leaders suited to take over for me?" It's the difference between making yourself better and making those around you better.

In chapter 9, we addressed people development in general. The three-step process we identified there applies to identification and development of future partners, as well:

- Identify what competencies you are looking for from this person based on the position he or she is filling at this point and what level of competencies you are trying to move him or her to in a nonequity partner position.

- Assess how well they are presently performing against these expected competencies.

- Develop action plans for training, educating, coaching, and developing them.

When it comes to the identification and creation of competency definitions, you can create them yourself, or you can use a competency model and framework already created for a CPA firm, such as our Succession Institute Competency Framework.™ Similarly, with respect to assessing how well someone is doing with respect to demonstration of expected competencies, you have some options to consider. For one, you can simply observe and make notes regarding critical incidents that show the positives and negatives of a person's performance (not our favorite approach). You can create an assessment form that the employee and others in the firm with whom they work complete to create some idea of their performance. Or, you can use a 360° performance assessment created by someone else, such as the Succession Institute Performance Assessment,™ which measures performance against the competency framework from which it was developed. The more input your partner candidate can obtain, the better, so having some sort of multidirectional assessment such as a 360° assessment can provide a robust view of how an employee is doing at any particular time. As well, use of a formal framework and related assessment creates more objectivity for the partner candidate evaluation process, and it provides a career path for your motivated professionals to pursue.

Action plans regarding development of partner candidates will likely include identification of formal and informal training and education, coaching, and mentoring; experientially driven job assignments; and opportunities to take on leadership roles in critical projects within the firm. There's already a variety of training options available that focus on the people and project sides of management, and we predict a growing number of these offerings in the future. For example, we work with multiple CPA firm associations and state CPA societies to deliver customized leadership development programs to their members. There are plenty of groups, from the AICPA to state CPA societies to CPA firm associations to CPA firm consultants, who offer a plethora of options to consider.

New Partner Admission

We recommend that once they've determined whether someone is suitable for joining the partner group, the firm brings him or her on as an income partner (nonequity partner) first. To the outside world and the rest of the employees, this person is a partner. Internally, to the rest of the partners, he or she is an employee being placed in a new role. Making people income partners allows you to see how those partners-to-be will handle themselves in the new role and with new responsibilities before things are complicated by having them buy in and become equity partners.

Some of you may feel you know a candidate well enough by the time this decision occurs that there's no reason to delay an equity buy-in. We can entertain you with multiple stories of (anonymous, of course) high performers who were exemplary in their positions prior to becoming partner, but then became different people once they had "Partner" on their business cards. We have seen people admitted as income partners who were able to leverage their role and start bringing in business, and we have seen others do nothing other than what they did as managers. This is one important behavior to monitor when evaluating an ownership offer. But to us, some of the most important characteristics to observe are whether the new income partners share their opinions during the partner meetings, who they put first in their decisions—themselves or the firm, whether they use their new power in the firm or abuse it, whether they are trustworthy, and more. At the end of the day, to become an owner, a perfect storm has to occur. First, there has to be a need for another partner (growth, potential, and so on). Second, the potential partner needs to display the competencies required to perform the job of partner. And third, this person needs to embody the qualities, characteristics, and values of the firm. Admitting someone as an income partner for a few years gives the owners clear insight into whether these conditions are being met.

We recommend that you normally require someone to work as an income partner for a couple of years before you make the mutual decision that the privilege of being an equity owner has been earned. Certainly, there are plenty of cases in which a year or less is plenty of time to make this transition. But even more often, some income partners never become suited for equity ownership. Don't establish an expectation that once an income partner has served a specific amount of time in that role, they will be automatically admitted as owners. The message needs to be simple: Equity ownership requires three achievements: demonstrated competencies, proven personal qualities, and a need on the part of the firm.

It should go without saying that anyone in the position of income partner should be tied to an employment or partnership agreement that contains penalty provisions if they choose to leave and take clients or staff with them. We recommend liquidated damage of 200 percent of client fees and salaries of staff taken.

Admission to Equity Ownership

Assuming a need by the firm, an income partner who has shown the required level of performance against the competency framework and proven qualities would be admitted as an equity owner. One of the questions we frequently hear is, *What would a fair buy-in be?* We see a wide range of practices in this regard. For example, we have seen partners buy in at full price (based on overall firm value derived from total firm revenue and the percentage of ownership they're acquiring).We don't like that approach because when you make people buy in at full value, if they suddenly decide to leave, which could be as soon as two or three years later, they'll want to be bought out at full value. It creates an undesirable set of circumstances. One of the main benefits of bringing in younger partners is to make sure they are still around to take over when it is time for the senior partners to go.

Therefore, we prefer to see younger partners buy in at accrual net book value and be required to stay long enough to earn a fair market value buyout that they've built, essentially, through some sweat equity. The big payoff for younger partners needs to be tied to them staying and performing over the long run until, age-wise, it is time for them to step down and let the next generation of partners take over. We recommend that new partners be sold from 3 percent to 5 percent of equity when they first come on as owners. Usually, with today's capital requirements to fund and operate a firm, this is a significant enough amount that new owners feel they have some skin in the game. We also recommend that to strengthen this "skin in the game" commitment, some portion of their buy-in price be paid in with their own money, such as $25,000 (or more depending on the size of the firm). The balance due for the buy-in often is paid through withholding from salary increases and bonuses over five years, with interest paid on the balance.

Nurturing New Partners

If you want your partners to be able to take over when you leave, you need to invest in small losses now and let them learn how to lead while you are still around to help them avoid big mistakes. In other words, let them make mistakes commensurate with their positions. Firms need processes that force these younger partners to formalize their exciting new ideas into a business plan model that challenges them to think through everything from service launch, marketing, talent development, and service delivery to client satisfaction within a planned timeframe and budget. This requires infrastructure—something few first generation firms are willing to invest in and put in place because the founding partners just do what comes naturally. It also requires deliberate, aggressive training and development of your people at a level that too few firms currently embrace.

Your people are the future of your firm. Firms must invest in them to help ensure that their succession planning is successful. Unfortunately, our experience and the succession planning surveys we've conducted over the last dozen years show that many CPAs aren't investing in the future. Now we are seeing some cases in which the senior partners are expressing a sincere interest in helping their junior partners learn some new skills. This is definitely good, but sometimes that's as far as it goes. Often, the senior partners believe that all they need to do is train and "fix" the junior partners, and everything will be just fine. The problem with this line of reasoning is that the senior partners often need to learn (and apply in practice as changed behaviors) as much about people management, interpersonal skills, delegation, and communication as their junior partners; but the senior partners take the position that they don't need to change—everyone else does. We believe, and have proven to firms over and over, that it's never too late for anyone to learn a few new skills and approaches.

Additionally, how many times have you or somebody you know come back from some eye-opening training and tried to apply it back at the office with little or no success? That's another common problem. You can't continue to operate in "we've always done it this way" mode and expect a junior partner to come back and achieve any significant transfer of skills learned in training. The way you've always done it will stand in the way of ongoing, active, practical learning and development. Stated differently, you need to clean up your practice to allow the remaining partners the opportunity to develop their strengths while the practice continues to grow profitably.

Under the Success Mode of operations (chapter 4), founding fathers are looking for their replacements to be images of themselves and believe they shouldn't have to train anyone—no one trained them! Besides, if talented leaders don't emerge on their own, then they will just sell the firm out from under the other partners.

Under the Continuation Mode of operations, every partner, every manager, every senior, and every junior staff member is working on developing their replacement. Succession and transition isn't about a few key positions at the top, but about filling positions everywhere. For anyone to move up in an organization, someone has to be ready to step in and take their place. Developing your replacement in this mode is not something employees do when someone is a couple years from retirement, but something everyone understands is part of their annual job responsibility. It is a simple philosophy: If you want to move up, you need to have someone ready to take your place.

Dead Weight

No discussion of changes required for your firm to be succession-ready and tee up an internal transfer would be complete without addressing the issue of dead weight partners and employees. Most of us have probably had the misfortune of working with someone like the character Wally in the Dilbert comic strip. He's the guy who doesn't do much—doesn't add value, doesn't help others out when they need a hand—in short, someone who's not pulling his weight and may even be detracting. You, as a strong-willed entrepreneurial owner, may have been able to manage your Wally over the years and get enough production to justify his or her position, but when you're gone, it is unfair of you to leave this mess to the remaining partners to manage. They already have enough to transition when replacing a senior partner, and they don't need the additional burden of dealing with dysfunctional people who should have been terminated long ago. To make matters worse, sometimes your Wally will have garnered over the years more power and authority through his equity rights than he deserves or has earned (if you haven't gone through an equity reallocation process, see chapter 7). This makes him an even more formidable problem for the younger owners to deal with.

If you have partners who are not acting like partners, who avoid client relationship-building like the plague, or who don't want to be held accountable, get rid of them now. If you have managers who are not pulling their weight, who, at best, are not running any good clients off, but at worst, are not doing anything to help cement client relationships and are not lifting a finger to develop others in the firm, get rid of them now. Don't saddle the remaining partners with inadequately skilled people who don't care enough to get better or who refuse to change their behaviors for the good of the firm. If the first step the next generation of owners has to take to run the firm profitably enough to pay you off is to terminate marginal partners and managers, then we can tell you one thing for certain: You need to be taking a deep discount in what you are being paid for your value in the firm.

The tone is set at the top of an organization. Do you want to create and maintain a professionally challenging and rewarding culture centered on client service, problem solving, and adding value? Or do you want to create and maintain a culture centered on lack of accountability and no consequences, characterized by comments such as the following:

> "At least he is a body and gets some work done."

> "She is not very good, but better than nothing."

> "As soon as we hire enough staff, we will get rid of him."

> "She's a problem, but we have bigger problems to deal with right now."

The choice is yours. The preceding statements are common initial responses we hear when we suggest that changes be made. Short-term pain is often required for long-term gain, but it is well worth it. Do you think that the other, less senior people in your organization can't or don't see the inadequacy of performance and corresponding lack of consequences right now? How can you ever build sustainability on this kind of foundation? While you might be making a great living, we can only imagine how much more successful your organization could be if you would just address the dead weight at every position now.

We can tell you the outcome of procrastinating regarding this issue. Eventually, you will drive off your best people so that you can keep your marginal ones. That is a succession strategy we suggest that you avoid.

In Conclusion

Ultimately, you need to give up some power and control in order to allow what you are setting up to endure beyond you; and you want to do it before you leave so that you can still influence the organization while it is making its way through some uncharted territory. For many or most owners of CPA firms, retirement payout rests in the hands of those who follow them. Don't just leave your partners with long-standing deferred organizational and human capital maintenance when you depart. Give them a better chance for success with the opportunity to lead within a structure that makes sense for the future, not just what makes sense for you.

For many retiring entrepreneurs, the shift in ownership and control when they leave presents the most vulnerable, dangerous position their firm will face. The owner or owners on whom the firm has depended for key decision making will no longer be in a position to drive the firm and related outcomes. Without adequate advance preparation that includes installation of governance infrastructure and partner development for the incoming leadership, the firm and remaining owners will be operating at the edge of a crevasse, and a fall from that edge could be lethal to the firm. This truly requires adequate advance preparation and consideration, and although it's complicated at times, firms must address it.

There is no question that readying your next generation of leadership requires important developmental components, such as outside training, on-the-job training, mentoring, coaching, and constantly elevating trial-by-fire experience. Most firms we work with are starting to make good progress in this direction. The points we focused on in this chapter are those that are most often overlooked as changes are considered. If handled properly, they will be significant steps forward toward operating in Continuation Mode at your firm. Too often, the discussion among the senior owners is about the inadequacy of the firm's next generation of leaders. The point we want to drive home is that in our experience, the disconnect is less about their abilities and more about the overall situation they inherit, including what you are doing to prepare them to take over. This is all easily fixable, but it requires you to address this now and confront the issues you know need to be resolved.

Chapter 12: Build a Strong Partner Group

Turnover Basics

Now that we have talked about people buying in, a logical next step is to talk about people leaving. This chapter is focused on voluntary or involuntary withdrawal from the firm, which includes benefits available when leaving and competing or not competing with the firm, penalties for leaving and taking staff or clients, and the vote required to terminate a partner. As we have said several times throughout this book, your firm should not be in the business of creating spin-off competitors. This chapter addresses some basics of handling the ebb and flow of partners in a CPA firm.

Cranking the Vise

Why is it that partners don't have a philosophical problem with the idea that our people (managers, supervisors, seniors, staff, administrative, and so on) should be managed, but at the same time, believe that partners don't need that same oversight? The entire time today's partners were developing as employees, they were managed by someone. They were being held accountable for meeting certain performance standards. But, a common theory is that once you become a partner, supervision isn't necessary because you know all you need to know to direct and manage yourself. From our viewpoint, that perspective is clearly flawed, and we are not alone in our thinking—accountability has consistently been a top issue for CPA firms, according to the AICPA's PCPS Top Issues Surveys.

So, how does this relate to the subject of this chapter? It is simple. First, you need to set expectations for everyone in the firm, including partners. Then, you need to hold everyone, including partners, accountable to those expectations. As firms grow, more and more systems, processes, and procedures are implemented to ensure consistency, quality, appropriate client service, and more. When staff won't comply, firms usually fire them (after about two years of noncompliance); however, when partners won't comply, unless a partner has done something unethical or egregious, it is common for the rest of the partners to just complain about them year after year without solving the problem.

With this in mind, a partner does deserve more room to recover than non-partner staff because a partner has had to achieve a great deal in the past for the privilege of being asked to join the ownership ranks. So, when a partner isn't complying with expectations, systems, processes, or procedures, then a talk needs to occur between the partner's boss, usually the managing partner, and the rule-violating partner. If that discussion doesn't instantly change behavior, then the vise needs to be tightened to apply more pressure. The best way to do this is to penalize the partner financially for lack of compliance. If that doesn't work, then the boss cranks the vise even tighter by making the financial penalty more punitive. But if that doesn't cause the necessary changes to take place, then the firm needs to be ready to make the ultimate turn of the vise and let that partner go. Putting up with noncomplying partners year after year sends a clear message to everyone in the firm that its leaders can't be trusted. In this scenario, as leaders, our words don't mean much because at the end of the day, we don't say what we mean, we don't back up our words with action, and we discriminate by allowing certain people to violate the rules while holding others accountable to those same rules. So, for the sake of the firm's long-term viability, you have to have a way, and a willingness, to cut partners from the herd who have made it clear that they will not be managed or held accountable to the firm's expectations, systems, processes, and procedures.

Terminating a Partner

Let's first take a look at the simplest process, which is termination. Recognize that to get to this step, a firm has already gone through the process of tightening the vise and still doesn't have sufficient compliance by the partner, so it is time to take the vote to terminate.

The first problem many firms have is that the voting threshold required to fire a partner is too high. The second problem is an insufficient process for enlightening a partner about his or her critical failings, articulating next steps if improvement doesn't occur, and keeping the other partners in the loop of this counseling progression.

We recommend a voting threshold of a supermajority vote of the equity interest in the firm for terminating a partner. Terminating a partner should not be easy, but what we frequently see in practice is that it is entirely too hard. For instance, we have seen partner agreements that require a 100-percent "yes" vote from all the partners, even the partner being terminated, for the vote to pass. More liberal agreements, written in this same frame of mind, would require a 100-percent vote of the equity partners for termination with the exclusion of the partner being considered for termination. In either of these situations, it is almost impossible to fire a partner. Even rogue, self-serving partners are still likely to have another partner who is a good friend, or another nonperforming partner who will create an informal voting alliance to block any action with this level of consequence. Even agreements that call for an equity vote of 75 percent to 99 percent "yes" vote to fire often fall into the same category. When the voting threshold is too high, it simply takes too few votes to block termination as an action.

If the firm has gone through the vise-tightening process and the partner still won't comply, but the firm can't execute termination, then the firm lands at the worst place of all: where partners know that they can do as they please with no real consequences or accountability for their actions. Therefore, the supermajority equity vote of 66 2/3 percent is a good number from our vantage point. It is not an easy vote to obtain, but one partner (or, depending on the size of the firm, a very small minority of partners) can't block the vote, either. When partners challenge us about this while we are consulting for them, our comment is consistent: Although this lower threshold will make it easier to fire a partner, if 66 2/3 of the equity interest partners in this firm want you gone, why would you want to stay?

On the second front of insufficient clarity regarding the process, we address goal setting, accountability, and performance incentives in chapter 15 on partner compensation. That process creates a great deal of transparency. When combined with the processes described in chapters 3 (Clean Up Your Operations), 4 (Identify and Describe Your Business Model), and 6 (Describe Governance, Roles, and Responsibilities), the result should create a great deal of confidence within the partner group that a fair process is in place and that plenty of opportunities for reform are available should the partner in question desire to stay with the firm.

Leaving and Going to Work in Industry

We recommend that our firms take the approach that if a partner leaves, the firm ought not want to fight over whether that person can practice as an accountant. We would rather take the stance that the departing partner can set up shop right next door if they prefer, but he or she doesn't have the right to take any of the firm's clients or staff without paying damages for that hostile action. We are presuming that departing partners have decided that it is time to leave public accounting and might practice full- or part-time running their own business (not a public accounting business), work in industry, or retire; in any case, these partners are not interested in taking clients or staff with them.

In this case, the following conditions would exist (more details about the terms and conditions are shared in chapter 12 of volume 2). The withdrawing partner agrees to automatically and immediately sell his or her equity interest in the firm according to the following conditions:

- The partner will not be entitled to any undeclared or partial year incentive bonus compensation.
- The partner will be entitled to his or her capital or equity interest in accrual net book value according to the terms and conditions of the partner agreement.
- The value of a partner's retirement benefit for his or her equity interest will be determined by the terms and conditions of the retirement agreement (see chapter 5 for more details on determining the retirement benefit).
- The partner is subject to adjustments on any outstanding amounts owed based on compliance with the firm's client and referral transition process.
- The total amount due the partner will be offset by any outstanding liabilities owed to the firm by that partner.
- A listing of acts that will immediately cause discontinuation of any payment of deferred compensation.

The purpose of this type of policy is to make it clear to departing partners that any damage they do the firm will have a financial impact on the final dollars they receive from the firm. In other words, when a partner leaves, we expect that partner to give the firm adequate notice, properly transition clients and referral sources, and be an ambassador (or at a minimum, not be a detractor) for the firm in whatever new role they take on in the community.

Leaving and Competing

In this variation of leaving, the departing partner is clearly leaving with the intent to practice in the field of public accounting. As we mentioned previously, in our opinion, that is okay as long as that partner does not use his connection with the firms' clients and staff to motivate them to leave with him or her. However, because it is likely that some will leave, the firm includes a penalty that will be owed to the firm for this aggressive action against them. Our typical recommendation is for the departing partner to pay the firm two times annual collected revenues for any clients taken and at least two times the total compensation for any staff taken.

We believe that paying two times total annual compensation is not really a significant penalty for taking staff. Partners who leave rarely take your worst staff—they take your best ones. Finding someone to replace your good people is difficult and expensive because most firms have to hire them right out of school and develop them internally. As well, because the firm has lost critical capacity with this unexpected staff loss, the firm is likely to incur extra costs in overtime with existing staff, additional training and development time to get others up to speed, and possible headhunter fees trying to find replacements. It is for these reasons that some firms are starting to use a greater multiple, like 2.5 or 3 times annual total compensation, as the offset for a departing partner taking staff. On the off chance that partners take marginal staff with them, consider waiving the staffing penalty or providing a discount for a particular person or two (get creative in your explanation about why). Otherwise, if the price is too high, the firm may convince the departing partner to leave that marginal staff member with them.

As for taking clients, as we said previously, two times fees is our recommendation for any liquidated damage calculation. We justify this penalty with the fact that the reason a partner has a strong enough connection with a client to motivate that client to move with the departing partner is because of the partner's access to, and awareness of, that client's personal and confidential data. Most firms don't have a penalty for this action, but of the firms that do, it is more customary to see one times fees as the penalty. Our response to this is that if the market price for buying a partner's book of clients is one times annual fees based on retention (EWYK model of operations), and given that the departing partner is hand-picking the clients he or she wants to take, it stands to reason that retention is probable. In this situation, why would any firm set up a policy that motivates young managers and partners to build relationships with clients while being paid by the firm to do so, use the firm's reputation to gain access for developing new client relationships, then leave and be able to cherry-pick their best clients and only be charged market value for that hostile act? We call this strategy the "incubate your competition" strategy, which we recommend avoiding at all costs. By this reasoning, we believe two times annual fees is not punitive—simply fair.

The rest of the process dealing with partner withdrawal, besides the addition of penalties or liquidated damages for taking clients or staff, emulates the process described previously for partners leaving and not competing.

Other Issues

Employment Agreements

These policies regarding partners leaving with or without taking clients or staff are commonly locked in through the firm's partner agreement. However, for non-partners, we recommend covering some of the same basics through an employment agreement. Based on commentary from numerous attorneys we have worked with, some form of remuneration needs to accompany the execution of employment agreements for them to be valid. Therefore, we recommend incorporating the adoption of this into your firm's next annual bonus and salary adjustment process so you have a quid pro quo for partners signing the agreement. We recommend that the firm work with its attorney as soon as possible to put this important firm protection agreement in place for any non-partners who are, or will be, working directly with clients and building relationships with them.

Total Loss of Retirement Benefits

Some firms, especially larger firms, have clauses in their partner agreements declaring that any partner leaving and competing with the firm is not entitled to *any* deferred compensation benefits even if they would be deemed to have earned those benefits had they retired under different circumstances. This is a choice each firm needs to make. In our approach, if the partner leaving is going to take clients, then the firm is made whole through the liquidated damages it will receive for clients or staff taken. However, as many have found through litigation over these types of matters, the courts and arbitration can be very fickle in their interpretation of "fair." Therefore, by removing the right to earned retirement benefits if the departing partner is leaving to compete with the firm, at least the firm isn't losing clients or staff while also having to pay retirement benefits if, for some reason, the courts rule that the departing partner does not have to pay the agreed-upon penalties for taking clients and staff. We believe that penalizing a departing partner for the fees we recommend for clients and staff taken and canceling their earned retirement benefit seems excessive. On the other hand, allowing a departing partner the possibility of being paid a retirement benefit and being permitted to take clients and staff to compete with the firm is a recipe for the firm dissolving and going out of business.

Terminations for Cause

It makes sense for the firm to identify actions or circumstances in which partner termination is instant and clear. Our advice here is to not try to catch your bad partners through this policy, which we find is a common failing. When your firm sets up the policy (and we recommend this thought process for all policies you create), consider that your strongest partner is the one that might end up violating it. If you absolutely believe that the partner group will enforce this policy when your strongest partner violates it, then you are taking the right approach. What we often find is that firms create a policy to catch a specific partner doing something the partner group expects them to do. The problem is, the wrong partner is the one who typically gets caught in the trap. More information on typically listed "for cause" actions or circumstances driving termination is outlined in chapter 12 of volume 2.

Severance Packages

We also recommend putting together a standard severance package for departing partners, managers, and so on. We think of this as a clean-up provision that outlines some basics that need to always be taken care of in departure situations, including

- confidentiality regarding the transaction itself;
- confidentiality regarding firm data;
- rights, or lack thereof, of the departing partner regarding work product and intellectual capital;
- return of property (keys, firm technology, files, and so on);
- repayment of unearned compensation;
- non-disparagement of the firm;
- stipulation that everyone agrees to this resolution and transaction; and
- liabilities for past actions, should claims arise.

This severance package might end up costing the firm a couple of extra months of pay (or whatever variation of this amount—less or more—than your attorneys suggest is appropriate for the level of person leaving), but it cleans up the transactions, commonly shuts down nuisance litigation, and most important, builds in a short timeframe to wrap up all of these sloppy issues that can otherwise seemingly linger on forever.

In Conclusion

Termination is an important process to clarify and be transparent about if you want to build a robust succession plan. We believe that one bad apple can spoil the whole bunch. It is critical to have a reasonable way to cull those partners who really don't want to be part of a team and who would rather use the team when convenient, but fly solo the rest of the time. To be clear, this isn't about culling bad people. It is about being able to cull partners who don't play well with others, who don't want to be accountable to the firm, who won't put the firm first in their decision making, who can't seem to respect or follow firm strategy, and so on. This, in our opinion, doesn't describe a bad person; it simply describes someone who likely needs to be on his or her own because they are unwilling to fill their role as one partner within a group of partners.

Chapter 13: Establish Processes and Procedures for Retired Partners Still Working for the Firm

Continuing to Work After Sale of Ownership

More and more CPAs are continuing to stay active and work past normal retirement age. As you know, we recommend that a mandatory sale of ownership (MSO) normally occur somewhere around age 65–67. With the ongoing increases in longevity and personal productive capability, it is not uncommon for some professionals to want to work past the age of 65—sometimes, far past it. In our opinion, as long as the retired CPA partner has sold their equity interest, remains professionally able to do the work, and wishes to continue working with the remaining partners with their mutual consent, we don't see a problem. Nonetheless, there needs to be some clear boundaries established for this to work successfully for both parties.

Boundaries Are Necessary

To give you an idea about some of the boundaries we recommend, consider the findings from our succession surveys. Some interesting facts have come to light. For one thing, less than half of firms limit the involvement or influence of retired owners in the firm's operations. We believe categorically that retired owners should have no involvement or influence in firm operations; they should not be members of leadership groups, nor should they be attending board or management meetings. Remember that the reason for MSOs is to allow the *next generation* of owners to take over and run the business. If, for instance, retired partners are still attending management meetings, they typically will not stay quiet and will all too often try to influence decisions just as they did when they were part of the core leadership group. We've experienced many retired partners with personalities so intense that they either railroaded meetings they attended or stifled the conversation altogether when the topic was one of which they didn't approve. Surprisingly to us, this would happen even when those previous owners didn't have the right to vote or have any legal say in the final decision. We recommend setting up processes and expectations that allow the firm to utilize the skills of the retired partners but keep them out of strategy and management discussions unless a specific topic warrants their opinion. However, even then, the firm needs to bring in a retired owner for their opinion due to his or her unique expertise, discuss the issues, and then nicely dismiss the retired owner before the partner group brings any issue up for a final vote. It is so much better to make it clear, tactfully and consistently, that while the partner group respects the opinions of the retired partners, the processes in place preclude any chance of those partners being involved in the final decision.

If a retired partner continues to work at the firm either in a full-time or part-time role after MSO, it should be in a back room capacity, with no client relationship management duties. Retired owners should not manage client relationships. Period. They are supposed to have transitioned these relationships to others in the firm so that the firm can maintain a continuous income stream from which to pay them. Some firms make an exception to this rule to allow a *nominal* amount of revenue to continue to be managed by the retired owner, made up of clients who are (1) specifically identified, (2) very small clients (no large clients), (3) long-term friends or family of the retiring owner, and (4) not deemed important to the firm. *Nominal* in this sense, for example, might mean that the aggregate revenue from these clients would not exceed $20,000 to $30,000 or so, depending on firm size. Outside of this kind of exception, retired owners should be allowed to only work on other clients as a manager, with another partner handling the client relationship.

In our opinion, examples of activities that make sense once a partner transitions to a retired partner employee status include the following:

- Goodwill ambassador for the firm in its market, keeping the name of the firm out in the community, making contacts, and referring business in to the firm
- Technical reviewer or preparer (technical manager role) within the firm
- Delivering consistent, thorough, technical training for higher-level employees
- Improving the quality of processes within the firm

Given that the real job of management is to develop their people and build a stronger firm, although the retired partner employee can have a definite role in training and process improvement, he or she should probably avoid direct personnel management and supervisory responsibilities except when acting as a project manager. It is best to leave the personnel development up to the people who will have to live with the end products of their supervisory efforts.

Sometimes, we hear of firms that wish to have a retired owner take on some firm administration. This can be good and bad. On the positive side, a retiring owner who's been involved in firm management or administration could probably step in and perform this work quite ably if there's a need that is going unfulfilled. On the negative side, though, how much are the administrative tasks worth in the marketplace, and is the retired partner employee going to be able to accept what likely will be a lower rate of pay and status for this kind of work? Also, it may sound simple to keep the firm administration function separate from general management, but how do you really keep the retired partner out of this influential area or avoid the appearance to the rest of the owners that the retired partner is still driving management decisions? Although we don't recommend this, it can be done, but it is tricky, and it takes a specific personality match to pull it off.

In summary, with respect to boundaries and contract specifications for retired owners, they shouldn't do what we see all too often: continue to do what they've always done, just working less hours, managing client relationships, managing people, and having a say in firm operations. Retired owners should be just that—retired owners. If firm management and the retired owner agree that the retired owner can still add value to the firm, then this agreement should be delineated in an annual contract that expires at year end. Unless a new contract is presented prior to year end, the retired owner then understands that it is time for him or her to pack up and plan to play a lot more golf (or something, but it won't work as usual at the office). Additionally, we strongly recommend that the retired owner understand they are not staying on filling a partner-level role but, rather, one more closely aligned to a senior manager or technical manager position. On another note, retired owners shouldn't continue to have the big office in the corner, either; they should be moved to an office more in line with that of a senior or technical manager.

Annual Contracts

If a retired owner is retiring on an amicable basis and a majority of the remaining owners believe that it's a good deal for the firm to employ that retiring owner to work on a full-time or part-time basis with the firm as established by vote, there's nothing wrong with allowing it under an annual contract (renewable only at the pleasure of the firm). This contract should spell out some specific duties and activities that retired owners can perform as well as and how they will be paid for performing those duties and activities. Without a required annual renewal of the contract, bad things often happen. Those allowed to stay around and work after MSO usually have a very loyal following among the partner group, or, conversely, have strong-armed their deal within the firm. In either case, it isn't uncommon to see a love-hate relationship between the retired partner and the remaining partners: The remaining partners really respect what the retired partner has accomplished; however, those same partners typically also want the retired partner to step into the background so they (the current owners) can spread their wings and take the firm in whatever direction they desire without conflict or criticism. Because of this love-hate relationship and the current owners not wanting confrontation and dissension from members of the old guard, we believe an annual contract is a required component of a good succession process.

There is often a great deal of baggage between the current owners and the retired owners; therefore, firms should define a process to mitigate possible conflict and confrontation about continued employment. The deal with a retired partner employee should be something like this: If we (the firm) don't actively renew your annual contract by the 11th month, then your contract will not be extended, and you should start working on tying up loose ends and packing up your office. Without this clear contract termination expectation, a retired partner might be asked to work an extra year with the intent of that being the only year, only to find that the retired partner doesn't take the hint that it is time to go. Many more years might pass before the current partner group gets so furious that they have an ugly confrontation and have to fire that retired partner. This shouldn't have to happen. Letting a retired partner go shouldn't cause this level of partner conflict. Although a retired partner might be disappointed when his or her contract isn't renewed, setting up the kind of simple system and communication we recommend will be far less ugly than the drama and trauma we commonly see. Remember, it is always far easier, albeit a little more confrontational, to outline a process at the outset, rather than trying to clarify everyone's positions after the fact.

On a positive note, when you have this type of arrangement between the firm and the retired partner, if the retired owner wants to continue to work, he or she usually will work much harder to make sure they are doing what the firm wants them to do. As well, they are much more likely to keep their nose out of firm operations, knowing that overstepping in this area is an almost guaranteed trigger for contract termination. Without this type of arrangement, the retired partner is likely to do exactly what they did when they were an owner until the situation blows up. For example, in a recent situation we observed, a partner was hired to stay on and be paid on an hourly rate to do specific work. This, in and of itself, was not the problem. The current partners had the expectation that he would get approval for the work he was doing. However, this person just did the work he wanted to do, including sitting in meetings and attending firm functions, and billed them for every hour he spent. This went on far longer than it should have (which is common because of the baggage we discussed previously) until the situation came to an ugly head. Set this process up right, with clear expectations and processes, and follow them to the letter with every retired partner. If you do, you will escape a great deal of damage that is absolutely unnecessary and avoidable.

Retired Partner Employee Compensation

If both the retired partner and the firm want to maintain a working relationship under a one-year contract, they'll need to set up a compensation system that makes sense for the relationship. Retired partners should not continue to be paid for a book of business after they retire (because they shouldn't have a book to manage), and we don't think that retired partners should continue under the line partner compensation plan as they did before they retired. In other words, all retired partners should be on a special retired partner compensation plan.

By the time a partner has become a retired partner employee, the retired partner should

- have properly transitioned his or her clients.
- no longer be managing clients (all clients who were assigned to them prior to retirement, except for the possibility of a few very small, nominal clients, should now be managed by the partners who were designated by the firm to take over the various client accounts).
- not be involved in the leadership of the firm or attending, unless invited to a specific meeting, any leadership meetings.
- not be competing with the firm by setting up shop somewhere else.
- be under an annual contract with specific terms and duties described. The contract should automatically expire each year. Without a renewal, the retired owner will know that their tenure working for the firm is over.

Common acceptable payments terms under an annual contract might include the following:

- Percentage of billings (working in the role of a technical manager). The percentages usually range from 25 percent to 40 percent. Paying the retiring owner in excess of 40 percent, which is often found in smaller firms, is excessive and provides the retiring partner a premium benefit. To be very clear, in this situation, the retired owner is paid a percentage of his or her personal billings, not the total project or client's billings.
- Percentage of first year's business for new clients, or in rare circumstances, new services. This number should be in the 10 percent to 20 percent range. Some

firms will pay 10 percent for two years; some will pay 10 percent to 15 percent for one year, but we believe that 20 percent in one year is too high. On the other hand, 10 percent for one year is normal and reasonable (adjusted for actual collections).

- Hourly agreed-upon pay for specific performance. In other words, specifically identified activities (networking, internal training, working specific referral contacts identified by the firm, involvement in charitable events or boards, and so on) can be paid on an hourly basis or set up as duties to be performed for a small stipend or salary each year. This would not be paid at a partner's billing rate but at a much lower internal rate.

- Other perks might also be considered, such as paying for identified CPE, licensing fees, an office (however, a manager-level office rather than a partner's office), expenses, and so on.

In Conclusion

As you can see, there are a great deal of policies that need to be put in place, significantly updated, or implemented with greater accountability to better position the firm for both the seamless retirement and management of the relationship *after* the retirement of an owner. No matter how painful these discussions might be today, they are not nearly as painful and economically damaging as they will be if you wait until someone is ready to retire, or worse, after they retire. When the discussions are early, or at least four or five years away from someone retiring, although arguments and emotions can run high, the conversation will be more about what is fair and reasonable from a business perspective. Once you get a year or so away from an owner retiring, the dialogue feels more personal, more about what the person retiring deserves rather than what is fair and sustainable for the firm. So, have these conversations now and work them out.

Chapter 14: Define the Maximum Payout Process and Other Buyout-Related Issues

Personal Liability of Remaining Owners for Retired Owners' Full Payout

According to our succession surveys, few firms (less than about one-fourth) require individual guarantees of the amounts owed to retired partners. If you think about this in the context of a one-firm business model, operating in Continuation Mode, it makes sense that personal guarantees would not commonly be required. The senior owners have often brought the junior owners into the business, they have set up the system of governance, and they have been influential in crafting every aspect of the firm's operational structure, from training and development to client mix and offered services. So, the partners taking over are working within the limitations or opportunities created by the retiring partners. If the retiring partners have done a good job, the partners will have no trouble staying together, and the firm will provide plenty of profit to pay off the debts of the firm. However, if the firm is held together by chewing gum and duct tape because of years of deferred maintenance by the senior partners, then saddling the junior partners with guarantees of the retiring partners' retirement benefit seems unfair. To put it another way, why would the younger partners commit to a personal guarantee for a business that operates exactly how the selling owners set it up, key players and all? If it fails, then the selling owners, in our opinion, had a lot to do with it.

Some reading this would respond, "If we sold the firm to someone else, we would demand that they personally guarantee the obligation, so why should it be any different for our existing partners?" Well, first of all, if you are the selling owner and you are demanding personal guarantees, you won't sell to any of our firms. We don't recommend it, and we don't see it. There are buyers who will make those guarantees, though, because when it comes to business, you can always find someone who will do something stupid. Most of the time we see personal guarantees executed within small firms when a single owner is selling part of the business to a new owner. Once again, we don't recommend that because those kinds of transactions get in the way of allowing the firm to grow to the next level. What we tell our owners is because you are deciding who to hire and fire, who will be a partner, and how your business is run, rather than demanding personal guarantees, start running your practice better. Asking for a guarantee from your partners is like saying, "Hey, I think the talent we have in this firm is untrustworthy and incompetent. I should know; I built it."

It is sufficient to say for now that most firms are bought without personal guarantees. Corporations with retirement plans don't guarantee those benefits, and we see the junior partners buying out the senior partners as more analogous to this type of payment. Most commonly, the retirement obligation is backed up by the full assets of the firm, but rarely is it additionally backed up individually by the partners. The retired owners have some recourse if they don't get paid; they can take back what was sold. So, our words of warning to the CPAs firm sellers are simple: Don't build a pile of junk for a business or you will likely get it back.

Specific Recourse or Cures Should a Retired Owner Not Be Paid in Full

On the face of it, you may believe that if you're asking a retired owner to work hard to assure a complete and effective transition of client relationships with a penalty for not transitioning clients properly, it's only fair to provide the retired owner with some recourse or cure if he or she doesn't get paid in full. Typically, we see that upon default of retirement payments, the retired owner will get his or her ownership interest back and will then sit in on owners' meetings and participate in owner group or board of director decisions. As you might imagine, a retired owner in this position would probably try to influence and micromanage the firm's business decisions, especially those of a more strategic nature, so our experience is that current owners are highly motivated and will find it in their rational self-interest to keep up with scheduled payments. We have seen firms break up prior to senior partners retiring because of the chasm between the expectations of value of the firm between the retiring and remaining partners was too large, and we have seen firms merge due to the same issues, but during our time working with CPA firms over the last few decades, we have yet to be involved with a default from an internal purchase.

Sale or Merger of a Practice

This two-book series is about how to set up your firm for succession from the current generation of leaders to the next. As we have stated many times before, we believe succession is easy if you run your practice well. So, regardless of whether you plan to sell your firm to your remaining partners, take the time to follow the steps outlined in these books because they will make your firm more valuable (more profitable) in the short run as well as in the long run (including in the case of the sale or merger of your firm). We tell our clients that whoever buys you or merges you in will take the same steps we have outlined in these books, from running off marginal clients to holding partners accountable to their roles and responsibilities, from establishing policies to enforcing them, from developing capacity at every level to closing competency gaps, and more. If the buyer has to do all of this because of your continual deferred maintenance, then they will either take their pound of flesh out of the value they ascribe to your firm, or they will run off your clients and people and only end up paying you for a portion of what you thought you sold to them.

Despite this warning, because selling your firm or merging it are possible outcomes you will be considering throughout the succession process, we have included coverage of these options in volume 2 due to its focus on the implementation of such transactions.

Ability of Retired Owners to Block Mergers or Total Sale of the Business Unless Retirement Obligation Is Paid in Full Prior to Transaction

Some retiring owners will insist on a provision that allows them to block the merger or sale of the practice unless their obligation is paid in full prior to the merger or sale. It's understandable that a retired partner would be concerned that his or her buyout could evaporate at a sale or merger conducted in the future. You might be thinking that for a retired partner to be able to block a sale or merger for a total cash-out on the front end seems unreasonable. Most sales or mergers have little, if any, front-end cash payments to the sellers involved from which to pay the retired partners in the first place. In fact, a merger or sale could actually strengthen the retired partner's position. We agree on the last statement; in many cases, particularly in upstream mergers, a merger could actually be better for the retired owners. However, consider a situation in which the current owners are merging to gain certain instant personal advantages. Although it is rare, it is possible that the current owners could make a lucrative deal on the backs of their retired partners. Or, consider another more likely scenario. The firm is in a small community, and the retired owner has a dislike and distrust of a firm or two in the area. Now that the owner is retired, the current partners decide to sell or merge with one of the retired owner's archenemies. Here is a case in which the retired owner, through sale or merger, would be forced to be a creditor for someone with whom he or she has a poor and confrontational relationship. To us, that isn't fair. In cases like this, why should the people financing part of the deal (those who built the firm and are being paid off for the value they created over time) have to live with whatever terms or agreements are made by the current partners regarding the disposition of the firm? If you were in the retired owner's position, would you be comfortable with this level of ambiguity regarding the viability of your payout?

From our perspective, if a merger or sale looks so good to the current owners that they can't pass up the opportunity, then one of two things should be easily managed:

1. The deal will be easy to sell to the retired partners to assure them of their full retirement payout.

2. The deal will be good enough for the remaining partners to justify a complete payoff of the retired partners.

Remember, paying off the retired partners is not an added expense for the firm, just an accelerated one. Paying off the retirement debt by the existing partners will add reciprocal value to what they would be receiving in their sale or merger transaction. Given this, for most firms (except very large ones), we recommend that your agreement be structured to allow the retired partners to block a sale or merger or to allow the partners to be taken out of the decision by paying them off. A good retirement benefit policy will have a present value calculation identified for early payoff anyway, so there is really no downside to providing this extra protection to those who have already served their time.

Ability of Retired Owners to Block the Sale of a Line of Business Unless Retirement Obligation Is Paid in Full Prior to Transaction

We believe that retired partners should be able to hold the firm accountable for a front-end cash payment from the sale of a line of business if that sale will significantly reduce the bottom line of the firm. Most retirement provisions carry a cap (see the text that follows) on what portion of net income will be paid to retired partners, so a material reduction in net income could have a negative impact on retired partners while the current partners line their pockets with cash from the sale of the line of business.

What qualifies as "material"? It depends on the facts and circumstances. The more retired owners you have collecting monthly buyout checks, the lower the threshold of materiality for changes in net income. Generally, we would recommend that the retired partners be able to block the sale of a line of business that represented something like 20 percent or more of the top line or 10 percent or more of the bottom line (the firm situation, size of the firm, number of partners, amount of debt owed to retired partners, and so on all affect where this line should be drawn). You could also have a provision that overrides the retired partners' ability to block the sale of a line of business if the entire sales price or a proportion of the sales price, net of expenses (that is, the total net proceeds), goes toward paying off the outstanding retirement obligation of the firm. This way, even if a sale represented more than 10 percent of the net profits, and even if the retired partners objected to such a transaction, the firm would not be restricted from consummating the deal as long as the retired partners received their proportion or greater of the available benefit. As we discussed previously, if something is a good deal, the existing partners shouldn't have a problem obtaining the necessary agreement from the retired partners to move forward. But even if the retired partners are being disagreeable, a provision like the one we just mentioned would take care of that. If the current partners are trying to access a windfall of cash and leave the retired partners out, then the deal deserves to be blocked.

Partially Funded Retirement Plans

Although we recommend 100 percent funding via insurance products for buyouts due to death, we don't recommend full funding for lifetime buyouts. When owners know that some portion of their retirement funding is already in place, it takes much of the pressure (pressure to do the right things for the firm) out of the succession process. Therefore, you don't want to fully fund retirement because this basically is creating a system in which the seller pays himself or herself in advance for the business and gives what is left of the business to the remaining partners. When retirement is fully funded, partners tend to stop doing what they should do to insure practice continuation because there is no risk or reward left for them. If your partner group feels some prefunding is important due to the conservative financial nature of your firm, you might consider partially funding (maybe up 15 percent to 20 percent or so) the near-term retirements to allow the firm a safety net to pay the retired partners in case the firm has an off year or two. This fund essentially serves as a back-up reserve to pay the retired partners in case of short-term problems, because the plan is to fully pay them from normal cash flow. However, it seems counterintuitive to us to suggest that a seller set aside money to pay himself or herself upon retirement. It's your money, and frankly, you get less of it because you deferred annual compensation years before only to get the same calculated retirement benefit, or less, paid with your own money.

Maximum Payout Provision

Because a firm needs to be able to maintain adequate profitability to pay the existing shareholders after the payment of the obligation to the retired shareholders, we recommend a policy that sets a cap in terms of the percentage of net income that can be paid to retired owners of a firm in any single year. We usually recommend something in the range of 12 percent to 15 percent of net income (net income being determined as all income available to partners before taking into account partner salaries, draws, or incentive compensation) as a cap on the amount that can be paid in any one year to retired partners. In our opinion, if a firm were to exceed that amount, payments to the retired partners could start to eat into the reasonable profitability of the existing partners. As the fable portrays, it is unwise to kill the goose that lays the golden eggs. The last thing retired partners should want to do is take away the desire of the existing partners to continue to work and support the firm. When there is not enough money left over after paying the retirement debt for the existing partners to earn a good living, they will be motivated to go to work for someone else or leave and start their own practice. So, the maximum payout provision is established to create a balance of paying the retired partners a fair portion of the profits while leaving enough to adequately reward those working to sustain those profits.

Some firms will calculate a cap based on gross income. We don't recommend this approach simply because it's too easy to manipulate gross income. As well, the caps we tend to see on gross income are often too high. Finally, given that gross margins for CPA firms range wildly, from 20 percent to 40 percent depending on the size of the firm and the economic conditions in a geographical area, setting a cap on gross income is an often extremely inadequate metric to determine a reasonable balance between the amount of money available to distribute to retired partners versus existing ones.

Purchase Price of Other Companies and Real Estate

Many firms spin off other companies because of the business environment. CPA firms might have a technology company, a wealth management company, or some other type of company associated with the accounting firm. We also often find CPA firms that buy their own buildings as part of their wealth creation strategy. Given these two common investments, when a partner retires from a CPA firm, there needs to be a mechanism to allow the firm to retire those owners from each of these other entities and investments, as well. Otherwise, it's unfair—somebody can retire from the CPA firm and continue to hold on to his or her ownership interest in these other companies or real estate while the existing partners maintain, invest, and grow them. As these companies grow over 5–10 years, those retained ownership interests can become very valuable.

Two problems are created by this scenario. First, the retired partner had nothing to do with the increase in value because he or she was not actively engaged in developing it, but without a policy addressing this, the firm has no way to remove the retired partners from these entities. The second is ownership conflict. As new partners are admitted to the CPA firm or as ownership percentages change within the CPA firm, we recommend that the ownership ratio in the CPA firm be identical throughout the other entities. Otherwise, you encounter the common situation in which the office building is owned by four partners, two of whom are retired and don't want to take any risk or decrease their cash flow, while the five partners in the CPA firm, three of whom don't have any ownership in the building, want significant investment in their office space or want to move altogether. Firms should set up their other companies and real estate in a way that requires partners to be bought out of all entities at the time of their retirement. As well, the ownership of those other companies and real estate should be constantly morphing to reflect the present ownership in the CPA firm. Failing to do this will create internal conflict that will continually undermine the core mission and business line of your firm. So, consider having a policy requiring partners to be bought out of affiliated entities and real estate when they retire from the CPA firm.

In Conclusion

If you approach the internal transfer of ownership in a fair and equitable manner using our recommendations in these books, you should be ready to begin transitioning your retiring partners effectively. Just remember that "fair and equitable" cuts both ways. The firm needs to be able to survive and thrive while paying off retired partners without the remaining partners having to toil endlessly to make it work. At the same time, the retiring partners need to be paid appropriately for their contribution to the successful business they have built.

Chapter 15: Create a Partner Accountability and Compensation Plan

Accountability: It Should Apply to Everyone

Accountability enables people who work together to trust each other's words, commitments, and actions. It allows team members to rely on one another to follow through on commitments and do what is necessary to ensure team success. Often, the problem is that this is a word used by people to describe how *others* need to be treated. For example, "It's time we hold *them* accountable," or "We need to put in a system that holds our people accountable for their work." In other words, it is an attitude of "What I am doing is fine; it's just that everyone else needs to be reined in, monitored, and punished when they don't live up to my expectations."

In his newest book, *The Overachiever's Guide to Getting Unstuck: Replan, Reprioritize, Reaffirm*, Bill Reeb talks about the inaccuracy of our perceptions. Here is an excerpt from that book that will clarify what we mean about accountability and those perceptions dealing with it.

> *We give ourselves credit for everything we think, say, and do.*
> *We only give others credit for what we see them do.*

This is a really important concept to embrace and one most people resist, so I am going to take you through a simple scenario. Let's say you had a project that had the deadline of last Friday. Because you were not done by 5:30 pm (your normal quitting time on Friday), you decided to stay late (until 9:00 pm) and get it done before you left. After leaving that evening, frustrated by this last minute requirement, you spent your drive time home and some time that evening pondering how this intense scrambling could have been avoided. Over the weekend, you found yourself continuing this mental dialogue and were excited when you came up with a few ideas worth trying to minimize the chances of this situation repeating itself.

On a different track, earlier that same week, you noticed a co-worker who was clearly struggling to meet a different project deadline. After surmising this, you extended an offer to stay and help if necessary. Your co-worker thanked you for your generosity, but declined the need for assistance. So, in this simplistic case study, you are likely to give yourself credit for the following:

- 3.5 hours of Friday evening work to get your project out on time,
- At least 1 hour of think time Friday night trying to come up with ideas as to how to avoid this situation in the future,
- A couple of hours of think time over the weekend to arrive at a couple of ideas worth trying to avoid this situation in the future,
- And bonus time for your willingness to stay and help out your co-worker, even though you did not actually stay.

Let me be clear. You deserve to give yourself credit for all of this effort and willingness. If you are like most of us, with each exceptional effort, you make a quick deposit in your imaginary "I Am Valuable" bank account. The bottom line is that for the week in question, you probably felt like you put in a minimum of six extra hours with a willingness to do even more, with the value-add of some creative efficiency ideas to boot. The problem comes when you compare your effort to that of, let's say, your co-worker who was in a similar situation (whom you offered to help). First, from a common overachiever's lens, you probably assumed that your co-worker only stayed for an extra hour or two maximum. Second, you might have diminished your co-worker's effort even further by thinking about how disorganized he or she was and had that been you with your superior skills, the late night effort would not have even been required. Third, no one else was the kind of team player you were and offered to help you. So, huge chasms are constantly being created in our minds when we compare ourselves to others because of our flawed and invalid perceptions.

How can there ever really be equity in our business or personal life when we always give ourselves credit for everything we think, do, and say and only give credit back for what we actually see others do? If this wasn't bad enough, we are likely to discount the effort we see from others with thoughts such as (1) they didn't put in the same level of caring or effort we did, or (2) they should put in more time given their lesser abilities as it takes them longer to do the same work we do. Even with what we see, our egos often get in the way of a realistic or accurate self-report as we inflate our efforts and diminish the efforts of those around us. As humans, we pay a lot of attention to ourselves, and don't pay that much attention to anyone else, so this contribution gap we hold on to as our excuse for not changing first is mostly fantasy.

Setting Clear Expectations to Create Accountability

Given this flawed view of those around us, it becomes clear that accountability needs to be rooted in much more than a casual perception, or it is destined to fail. Therefore, the first step to accountability is to move this from an observation and critique approach to one that clearly defines what you expect of someone upfront. This sounds fairly straightforward, and it is, but it is also loaded with plenty of traps to fall into. One of the traps to avoid is ambiguity. You can overcome this trap by taking time to describe the expectations you have of someone. Consider the following:

- What is the scope of work that you are expecting this person to do?
- What does the deliverable look like?
- How will we measure success along the way (and at what intervals)?
- What is the budget (time or dollars) for the work?

- When is it due?
- What resources are at the person's disposal to accomplish this project?

What we want to find is a situation with high accountability and low ambiguity. Unfortunately, most people don't take the time to lay out this information, so they end up with just the reverse—low accountability and high ambiguity. The odds of success in this situation are best described by what we call the Dirty Harry management approach (based on Clint Eastwood's famous movie character): Do you feel lucky today? When you have low accountability and high ambiguity, it will take a great deal of luck to obtain the results you are looking for.

Commitment to Results

Another idea to consider regarding accountability is the commitment to ownership of the end results. Accepting accountability is a commitment you make before the work is done, prior to knowledge of the end results. Accountability is easy to embrace when a project goes well. Even people who have nothing to do with a project will be glad to step in and be held accountable for good news, and this unfortunately happens more often than anyone would care to admit. But accountability really is about your willingness to take ownership of the future results, be they good or bad. If the results are bad, then put together your plan to fix them and start fixing them. Next, learn from your experience. If the results are good, don't just bask in the glory of your genius. Look to see what worked and why, so you can apply those pearls of wisdom to future projects. In other words, make an effort to learn from your successes as well as your failures.

Delegation or Dumping?

Next, don't dump—manage! Just because you were unambiguous about expectations and the person doing the work is taking ownership doesn't mean you get to walk away and then, at some point in the future, hold someone accountable for getting work done. You need to set up monitoring systems, processes, or specific checkpoints to get an understanding of what you are seeing and are not seeing to make sure the project stays on track. Accountability requires management oversight. You never get to walk away from your responsibility to monitor progress.

Monitoring does not mean to step in and micromanage. It means exactly what the word implies: You need to stay informed at a high level. That high level can easily be defined as knowing enough to see where the project is and enough that you wouldn't be surprised to find out various macro actions needed to be taken to complete it. We recommend, depending on the kind of work being performed, simple monitoring ideas such as a scheduled quick meeting to provide an updated progress report, a high level summary document journaling steps completed and steps remaining, feedback mechanisms like surveys or 360° assessments, or Gantt charts or to-do lists that can be glanced at to verify progress.

Revisiting the Notion of Accountability

When you consider that for many, the default definition of accountability is "our people taking ownership of our expectations without any involvement from us," it is easy to see why there are so many problems with achieving accountability. First, what do you mean when you say you want someone to "be accountable"? Second, what does "ownership" of work mean to you? Third, what are your specific expectations? Finally, if you don't need to be involved in the communication, setting expectations and oversight, just what role are you playing in this process? How can anyone ever be accountable when they are being judged based on performance requirements put together at the time of evaluation rather than at the time of project initiation?

Everyone wants accountability, but few people are willing to do the work to manage a system of this complexity. We are confused by the function of human resources versus human development. We think of evaluations as part of a compliance process rather than a key management tool to help improve those around us. We think that the administrative and training time required to teach people is lost production, and we think advancing our skills is a better use of our efforts than enhancing the skills of those who report to us. Accountability is something we can all achieve in our organizations, but it often has to start with changing the way we think about this subject, and usually, changing our culture to consistently spend a little time every day making sure the organization we are building for tomorrow is better, faster, and stronger than the one we have today.

Accountability for Partners

Let's take a closer look at what accountability might look like. We'll start with the partner group and then work our way down to the staff. For partners, accountability is best described as having a system in place that rewards partners for following processes and procedures, living up to their roles and responsibilities, and implementing the firm's strategy. On the other side, it provides sanctions when partners don't perform the preceding tasks. Rewards usually take the form of public praise, financial stimulus (incentive pay), and promotions (from non-equity to equity partner, being appointed to coveted committee assignments, and so on). Sanctions can include private reprimands, reductions in pay, and greater reductions in pay and can end in job demotion or termination.

The goal of accountability is to motivate everyone in an organization to work toward the goals and objectives established by the organization. The hope is to be able to use positive reinforcement to reward those acting in accordance with, and exceeding, expectations. However, experience dictates that it is equally important, even if only as a deterrent, to clearly identify sanctions for the lack of compliance or marginal performance. These sanctions often take the form of income losses or reductions.

In our way of thinking, accountability has to be firmly entrenched in ideas and ideals such as the following:

- Each partner should know exactly what he or she is accountable to perform.
- Whenever practical, each partner's accomplishments or progress should have some form of an objective component attached to help measure or monitor the results.
- Partners should be able to assess easily whether they are meeting or exceeding expectations.
- Expectations should remain constant and not shift to fit performance. There are circumstances in which performance expectations can shift, but these drivers should be out of the control of the person being measured (major economic shift during the assessment period, major health issues, and so on), not just because

management wants to avoid an uncomfortable discussion, an unhappy partner, or the stressful role of administering whatever sanction a partner earns.

- It is up to the individual partner, not the managing partner, to ensure that the proper levels of output are achieved.

- It is up to the managing partner to monitor performance, report to that partner (and at some point, to the board) on perceived levels of accomplishment, offer resources to provide assistance, and enforce the agreement, but *not* to ensure performance. If the managing partner's job is to ensure performance, then the partner is no longer accountable. (It's the managing partner's fault that the partner did not perform as expected, however.) In other words, the partner should be receiving exactly what he or she has chosen to earn based on the upfront agreement.

- Although personal growth goals can be customized to stretch each individual's capabilities, performance measures should be set at a level such that, in a normal year with a reasonable effort, they all will be met and exceeded. Therefore, by definition, performance goals should be established in a way that allows *very good* or *exceptional* effort to be classified and rewarded as *over*achievement.

- Consistently achieving less than the organization's minimum level of performance means that the partner won't get to keep his or her job at some point. This is a good sanity check for performance expectations. Just ask yourself this question when putting together a partner's annual goals: "If the partner I am assessing falls short of these expectations regularly, would I be comfortable asking the board of partners (directors) to demote or fire this partner?" If the answer is "Yes," then we believe you are approaching this correctly. If the answer requires a longer response such as, "No; while the partner should do better, consistently falling short would never bring about that level of action," then maybe you are setting your expectations too high. That is why you can't take action; although you would like to see the partner achieve the goals, falling short really doesn't mean anything, either. Remember, under this model of accountability, we expect everyone to meet their performance goals because they are hardworking, firm-focused, qualified partners. (If they don't have all of those qualities, then why are they partners?) Therefore, it is easy to see why we also expect the performance of many partners to significantly exceed the goals we are setting, earning them even greater rewards.

Accountability Requires Action and Commitment

Accountability is not passive. It usually requires a change in the philosophy of corporate and CPA firm cultures. It demands that partners (and employees), not management, be and feel more empowered regarding their performance. It is up to the partners to live up to the expectations of their jobs, affect how much they earn, determine how much work product they produce, and so on. It is up to management to become the resource to help those who want to help themselves. If a partner wants to perform at just the minimum standard or expectation, that's fine. Don't kid yourself; the minimum expectation level of accomplishment should be "satisfactory" and, therefore, represent a good level of performance. This satisfactory level of performance should earn a base wage and maybe even some amount of incentive pay. From that point up, the more employees accomplish, the more they earn.

Accountability and Performance Variability

An important point to keep in mind is that we, as human beings, have good months and bad months, good years and bad years. What is going on in our personal lives has a lot to do with how we perform in our professional ones. Therefore, if someone is going through a difficult time, such as a divorce, death in the family, or major conflicts with extended family, we can expect those events to spill over into his or her work life. Good performance systems allow people to have good years and bad years, with the result simply being a change in pay. In the good years, if the organization is doing better, it can share that gain with those who had the greatest hand in creating that success. Even when the organization has achieved about the same or worse regarding its overall performance, when one person performs exceptionally, that effort is usually making up for someone else's shortfall. In essence, good performance systems allow and support the natural ebbs and flows of our productivity.

Objective Performance Criteria

Objective, quantitative expectations are easy to process. If you expected a partner to bring in $150,000 of new business (with the assumption that this number is based on a satisfactory performance level, not an outstanding one), then the question is simply about how much business the partner brought in and how that compares to the goal. If the partner brought in $250,000, then clearly, overperformance occurred. If a partner brought in $100,000 in new business, then the partner clearly underperformed. We will get into how these two different actions might be treated under incentive pay systems later. For now, the point is that with objective criteria, it is fairly easy to assess the level of accomplishment. A few common examples of objective criteria, both financial and nonfinancial, in addition to new business are as follows:

- Additional services to existing clients
- Substantial increase in fees for the same project
- Profitability of client work
- Profitability of a department
- Billable or collectable hours
- Leverage of work being done (ratio of partner to staff work)
- Book of business managed
- Client satisfaction goals
- Total billings
- Write-offs
- Realization
- Collections
- Lunches or other meetings for staying up to date with clients
- Lunches or other meetings for staying up to date with referral sources
- Networking events attended
- Speaking engagements to promote the firm

Although this list just scratches the surface of possible metrics, it shows that assessing whether any number of these is accomplished is fairly straightforward.

Subjective Performance Criteria

On the other hand, subjective, qualitative criteria can make the assessment of achievement much more difficult. Training and development goals, delegation goals, and proper client transition goals are all examples of a more subjective expectation. In cases such as these, we need to come up with some form of objective support tool to help us assess progress. For example, to assess delegation, we might ask the employee to keep a diary of projects or work tasks that they have performed in the past that the partner delegated to someone else. We might then, on a monthly basis, sit with that partner and discuss the delegation experience, whether the proper monitoring was performed over the newly delegated task (in other words, was it actually delegated or "dumped"), and so on. Regarding training, we might survey the employees being trained at the beginning of the year and then a couple of times throughout the year to see how they feel about their training experience. We might ask for a development plan for each of the people the partner is responsible to improve and then discuss at specific intervals their assessment about the success of the training implementation.

Even with subjective criteria, we need to devise systems that allow us to catch people doing what they committed to do. Performance management is about putting systems in place that support personal evolution and success. It is about a structure that allows the people you are evaluating to demonstrate their progress over time, with ample opportunities along the way for you to provide insight, guidance, and resources when necessary. Unfortunately, most people implement performance systems that are only visited twice a year—when they are created and when it is time for the final assessment. These systems, while requiring less effort to implement, are often not even worth the time invested in them because they are not designed to help people meet and overachieve their expectations, but are simply in place to allow someone the ability to subjectively, and with limited knowledge, judge others.

Establishing the Accountability Process

Setting up an accountability and goal process always sounds much easier than it actually is to implement. For those who already think this process would be painful, just know that you still are probably underestimating the amount of agony in store. This leads us to the standard question, "If this is so awful, why would anyone do it?" The answer is both simple and abstract. The simple part of the answer is that, any time a firm can get all its key people working as a team toward the same objectives, the firm's chances of getting where it wants to go and achieving the success it desires are infinitely better. The abstract part of this is usually alluded to by this sort of comment from partners: "If all my key people are conscientious, hard-working, and share a common vision, shouldn't we be able to get to the same place without all of this extra administrative hassle?" Generally speaking, the answer is "no." In our experience, you won't get where you want to go consistently without this extra administrative hassle, especially as you grow larger. Recognize that this change in required administration oversight is a function of success. Sooner or later, your firm will outgrow the honor system of performance self-assessment and self-alignment.

The most difficult piece of this process to buy into (which, for many, takes years of trying to improve performance every other way first) is that this is not about getting people to work harder, nor is this an effort to find a way to clone all the partners in the image of one or two of the founding owners. This effort is about ensuring that all partners, and often senior managers, operate above a minimum performance expectation, that each has a self-development plan, and that the sum of all of these senior people's efforts are tied together to culminate in the achievement of the firm's strategy. This is the quintessential process required to take a firm to a higher level of performance.

Benefits of Implementing the Accountability Process

So, you ask, if performance management produces such a positive change and success, why would anyone balk at committing the effort to do it? Most senior people in a firm are successful because they are self-motivated, self-driven, and self-directed. Please pay particular attention to the "self" part of those descriptors. Having a set of goals and someone to report to who is assessing your realization of those goals is perceived by most as a loss of freedom, privilege, and flexibility, and for many, this increased level of scrutiny is not worth the trade-off for greater accomplishment. These self-driven people commonly respond with the same message we just covered previously: If we are all working hard, are conscientious, and our efforts are directed toward the same strategy, we will end up in the same place. No matter how many times someone states this, and no matter how emphatically this idea is expressed, it is rarely true. Even for sole proprietors, whose organizations are run by one person who does whatever he or she wants, you might expect to see alignment with strategy in this scenario because the strategy is about the sole owner; and certainly, you would anticipate the highest level of performance. But again, it is rarely true. That is why it is so beneficial for a sole proprietor to have an outside coach or create an advisory group. The sharing of expectations and having someone to report to, even as the sole decision maker, consistently creates a higher level of performance.

Life poses new challenges every day. Our to-do lists get longer and longer. We often find ourselves getting to a point where we are spending all of our time just re-spinning plates on sticks and ensuring they don't fall rather than resolving anything or making progress. Having well-defined goals helps you stay focused and helps you decide which plates should be allowed to fall off the stick and break. This is a big benefit of the accountability and goal-setting process—to help you decide what not to do or what to walk away from.

Another significant benefit of the process is clarity of the specific actions desired. For example, let's say we have three owners, and all three of them agree that is it essential to grow the business. At a quick glance, it sounds as though we have synergy in strategy, and everyone's efforts should be in alignment, but once again, this is not all that likely (based on experience, by the way). We recall a case (actually, there are many we can describe with similar disconnects) in which the first owner wanted to grow to maximize his retirement pay, which was based on the revenues of the business. To him, all business was good business because revenue was the driver of his benefit calculation. The second owner wanted to grow the firm to make room for his family members. In this case, he was interested in adding people to create opportunity for his kids (son and daughter) to work for the organization and then find a place in management. His vision was for his kids to eventually take over the business. The third owner just wanted to make more money. He liked the high life, and growth to him was all about "take home pay."

Each owner, based on the "business growth" objective would work hard, be conscientious, and keep the firm strategy in mind, yet each would end up making significantly different decisions as to what was the best use of their time, effort, and resources. This doesn't even account for the fact that one of the owners was dead set against family members working together in his business. This example shows how the owners' disconnect regarding strategy was destined to create confusion, expectation gaps, and eventually, conflict. But even when a firm's strategy is clearly articulated in detail, establishing annual goals and frequently reviewing them one-on-one with partners will always produce better results than allowing everyone the luxury of interpreting for themselves the best use of their time, effort, and resources.

Who's in Charge?

Once the decision has been made to implement systemic changes to hold partners accountable to specific performance expectations rather just relying on everyone to put in a self-proclaimed "good day's work," the next battleground is determining who will be holding whom accountable. As we have said, everyone likes the idea that "I" will hold "me" accountable, but few like the idea of anyone else holding them accountable. So, the discussion always shifts to "let's have a group of people, like a compensation committee, hold us accountable." The reasoning is simple: If I get crossways with one person, I will pay a penalty for that action. As I add more people to the evaluation process, it is easier to find a friend or an ally who will be willing to overlook my infractions and fight for my benefit.

Anytime we hear that performance assessment will be a group function, if we had a loud aggravating buzzer, we would be sure to set it off.

A group or compensation committee makes a lot of sense for some firms with respect to some specific functions. It is not a question of whether your firm should have a compensation committee; it is more the question of its charge. First, remember that a compensation committee, if formed, is a committee of the board of directors (or board of partners and so on). It is not a committee that has unique dictatorial authority. In our opinion, compensation committees should be charged with the following:

- Development of the firm's compensation system philosophy or framework to be approved by the board
- Recommendation of salary adjustments to the board if there are base salaries or guaranteed portions of salaries involved
- Establishment of objective metrics and firm-wide incentives that will support the accomplishment of the firm's strategic plan
- The review and evaluation of the overall performance of each partner and the recommendation of the compensation for performance pay to the board based on each partner's achievement using the approved compensation framework and metrics

Notice that the compensation committee does the heavy lifting on determining base pay and general incentive pay based on the compensation framework and metrics, but the final recommendation still should be approved or ratified by the board.

What is not clear in the preceding description is the managing partner's role in this process. The general compensation framework guides all partners, but because each partner has strengths and weaknesses and each partner has different responsibilities and job duties, there needs to be a customizable set of goals assigned to each partner based on leveraging strengths, improving weaknesses, meeting minimum standards of performance across all competencies, and accomplishing those tasks that are uniquely the responsibility of a particular partner. For this, management by committee—yes, compensation committee—is a bad idea. The most significant and success-driving job of the managing partner is to manage the partners. If the managing partner directs a partner to accomplish something specific or change a behavior or attitude without material compensation to reward achievement or punish failure, there is virtually no way for the managing partner to consistently hold the directed partner accountable. The most common counterargument posed here is that the managing partner can work through the compensation committee to affect the same outcome. There are situations when this might work, but not because the system is designed to work; only because the specific people on the compensation committee and the managing partner have such respect for each other that they can overcome the dysfunction of the system in place.

Successful firms in the long-term put governance systems in place designed to succeed, regardless of who occupies the various roles, rather than build systems around specific people that quickly fail when there is a shift in talent filling those roles. To put this in very clear terms:

> The managing partner needs compensation rewards and sanctions that he or she alone determines for each partner regarding the specific, individualized goals set out for each partner.

Please recognize the difference between governance rights and privileges and common sense. For example, a managing partner should

- set clear goals for each partner,
- outline the goals at the beginning of the year,
- meet with each partner to discuss those goals, provide a current assessment of accomplishment, and offer guidance about where to focus additional attention to achieve the goals, and
- meet regularly enough (which would be, at a minimum, quarterly, often every other month, and sometimes even monthly) to provide the partner with insight into his or her performance, providing time to make course corrections so he or she can achieve those goals.

The managing partner's job is to help the partner achieve his or her goals, not just sit in judgment of the partner. A managing partner shouldn't:

- use their power for personal gain instead of what is best for the firm.
- use compensation to manipulate partners to vote a certain way, drive a wedge between certain partners, or fragment the firm into factions.

When a managing partner is not following common sense values and objectives, such as those outlined previously, it does not mean that the firm should dilute the power of the managing partner's position. Do not turn over the powers a managing partner requires to be effective to a compensation committee just because you have an incompetent managing partner. Rather, install a managing partner who will do the job as outlined.

It is one thing for a compensation committee to evaluate performance regarding objective criteria—those metrics that are approved as part of the overall compensation plan each year. It is entirely another to have a compensation committee assess a partner's individual performance against customized goals, which are often qualitative in nature.

It is not the job of the compensation committee to meet with each partner quarterly and assess progress. That function belongs solely to the managing partner. It is not the job of the compensation committee to regularly coach partners in behavior and developmental transitions; that function also belongs to the managing partner.

Performance Pay for the Managing Partner's Allocation

Therefore, it should clearly *not* be the job of the compensation committee to control all performance funding because some amount needs to be reserved for the managing partner to make clear that his or her assessment of individual performance throughout the year has enough meaning for partners to pay attention to those communications. It follows that a reasonable amount (which means an amount that would be perceived as a motivational amount) of performance pay be reserved for discretionary allocation solely by the managing partner based on partner goal accomplishment. We believe that this is not only reasonable but critical to the success of your accountability and performance management system.

However, most firms are against such reserves. There are two predominant reasons. The first and foremost is that someone in the past, usually a previous managing partner, had too much control over owner compensation, and that power was perceived to be abused. For this reason, partner groups fight the idea of going back to a system that includes any discretionary components.

To be clear here, we are not advocating that the managing partner have control over all the compensation. We believe that would be an example of excess power for that position. We do believe, because the job of the managing partner is to manage the partners, that he or she should have compensation rewards and sanctions to hold each partner accountable to their individualized goals.

The second reason most firms don't like this type of system is that partners simply don't want *anyone* telling them what to do. You might say it is the "So who died and crowned you king?" perspective. Most partners believe that because they have proven themselves over 10–20 years of performance before being named a partner, they have earned the right to do things their way, and people need to trust that the choices they are making are for the best for the firm.

The problem is that this perspective is riddled with flaws. For example, although we would agree that partners generally prove themselves over long periods of time through their performance, during that time, someone or some group was managing them. So, just because an individual is named a partner, why should they move from a managed environment to one with total autonomy? That doesn't make sense. If we have 20 years of good performance being managed, why would we stop doing something that has been working so well?

Another flaw is the assumption that partners will make the best use of the resources of the firm. Our compensation systems prove that idea wrong all the time. For example, assume that a partner compensation system focuses on the two most common variables for CPA firms: book of business and personal charge hours. Now consider that a partner has an opportunity to bring in new clients, although the work is at a very marginal rate. From the firm's perspective, this work will tie up scarce resources and provide minimal profitability, if any. From the perspective of the partner bringing in the work, he or she will have increased the size of their book of business, which is one of the two main performance metrics. Clearly, in this example, the partner would be motivated to accept work that is not in the best interest of the firm.

Another common scenario pertains to charge hours. If a partner is compensated for charge hours, he or she is being motivated to do a certain amount of chargeable work personally. Now consider that a partner has work queued up that he or she is about to do, and in this case, let's also assume that one of the managers with plenty of excess capacity, who also has the skills to do that work, is sitting idle. When partners have not overachieved their charge hour goals, they will be motivated to do the work themselves in order to meet their performance requirements. So, in our view, instead of doing the right thing by always passing down the work to the lowest possible levels to create leverage and free up partner time, they will choose to misuse firm resources. The compensation system in this scenario is motivating the partners to make the wrong decision—to ignore idle resources and do the work themselves rather than passing the work down and freeing up time to perform those tasks or functions that only partners can do.

In Conclusion

The problem with using examples such as we do throughout the book is that life isn't just black or white. Considering the most recent example, it actually might be a good idea, in very rare and specific circumstances, for a partner to bring in a deeply discounted project. For many firms, their survival rests on the partner group generating a certain amount of money, so we can't totally take our eye off of this metric. With every example, the odds are extremely high that we can give you a positive and negative consequence for any action taken. Therefore, the real message we are trying to convey is that often our own systems and processes provide counterproductive motivation and unintended consequences to the firm's overarching strategies and values. This, in turn, means that we can't just rely on each partner to make the right decisions in a vacuum with respect to what is the best use of their time and resources for the firm.

As past success and personal development continuously demonstrate, organizations operate more effectively when people are managed; and because partners are people rather than gods or superheroes, it makes sense that we put something in place to manage them, as well. In volume 2, chapter 15, we will go into implementation-level detail about a common compensation framework as well as provide you with examples of how managing partner goals might work with some sample action plans and metrics.

Chapter 16: Address Death and Disability in Your Buy-Sell and Retirement Policies

Now Is the Time

Although the thought of the death or disability of a partner is not a pleasant one, any succession plan, retirement agreement, or buy-sell agreement needs to address how the firm will handle payouts for partners upon death or disability. This is necessary to protect both the firm and the individual partners of the firm. This section of the succession plan and policies addressing these issues does not need to be particularly complicated, but it does need to be well-thought out and reasonable from a business perspective.

Policies Dealing With the Death of a Partner

We recommend that firms address this issue in their succession plan by developing a couple of policies that deal with the buyout of deceased partners. One of these policies should address the buyout and the payment for a deceased shareholder, and another that goes hand-in-hand with it should address acquisition of insurance coverage for shareholders or partners in the event of the need for a payment due to death.

Most of the time, when faced with the death of a partner, survivors go to great lengths to be fair to the decedent's spouse and heirs, often to the detriment of the firm. The approach we suggest for handling this often creates some initial anxiety when we begin the discussion with our clients because death is one of those issues about which people become, understandably, very sensitive. For example, often, the first thing that people think when there's a death in the firm is, "If somebody dies, we need to pay out the full benefits right away." It is at this time that we have to step in and remind the partners of the need to protect the firm. While it is terrible when a partner dies, it is even worse if that event puts the firm in such a bind that it has to fire good employees or has to break up because of generosity the organization couldn't afford. We recognize that, at the end of the day, this is about the partners' values and judgment, and that is what needs to drive the final decision. But we also recognize that someone has to be resolute in these situations, which is why we speak up on behalf of the firm to create a balanced dialogue.

We know it is our job to be the devil's advocate in this, and we don't believe that people deserve anything, except their capital back, if they retire or leave before they're vested. So, yes, if a partner is young and dies prior to retirement, then technically, the only thing the firm should owe that partner's estate is their paid-in capital. But we also understand that partners are most commonly friends and family, and, due to the hardship the family is going through, the firm needs to find a way to be a little more generous. Therefore, we like the idea of taking the deceased partner to a fully vested status at death, but then we also recommend that the firm discount that fully vested amount (remember, that is a gift because the partner should have only been entitled to receiving their capital back) by 20 percent to 50 percent based on various criteria, with those partners who are vested having a lesser discount over those who are not. Different firms use different discounts based on what they believe the organization can withstand under such horrible circumstances. Regardless, we advocate for a reasonable discount for the following reasons.

The first is to keep in mind that the firm likely will need to hold onto some portion of the fully vested buyout to make sure that it can pay for the additional and unbudgeted costs involved with finding somebody to take over the deceased partner's client service responsibilities. Next, consider that the firm will probably have to work some of the partners a lot harder than normal during a transition period to be able to continue delivering the quality and timely services that will allow the firm to retain the deceased partner's clients.

Also consider that the death of a partner typically generates a lot of lost time with everybody grieving over this person's death, which is going to again have an impact on the bottom line. With as tightly staffed as some smaller firms are in terms of capacity versus demand, the firm is also likely going to need to hire one to several people to replace this partner just to do the technical work in order to keep moving work through the queue. This is going to cost extra money, too. Finally, consider that the firm is likely to spend some scarcely available time and premium dollars to attract this talent quickly. Now to be clear here, we realize that we are talking about a deceased partner and that this is a very sensitive topic. As we said before, we believe in taking care of the partner and his or her family; but at the same time, we also need to establish policies that give the firm some room to not only pay off the deceased partner's estate but also allow the firm some of the resources necessary to cover the extra costs that this terrible event will generate.

Don't be afraid to fund these types of buyouts with insurance. We can't tell you how many times we've seen small firms that have been penny wise and pound foolish. They didn't want to spend some perceived big chunk of money on insurance because they didn't think this type of event would happen to them. When a partner from this type of firm does pass away unexpectedly without insurance, many firms are forced to do one of two very negative things (in terms of values). They either are forced to pay the deceased partner's estate virtually nothing because of the lack of available resources, or the partners are forced to put their firms at risk of sustainability by taking on a financial burden they are not positioned to handle. Both of these terrible choices can be averted with insurance.

For the firms that do insure their partners' buyouts, many of their agreements provide that the firm can use the insurance proceeds in any way it wishes. We don't care for this approach because it allows greed to motivate poor long-term decisions. We suggest that firms consider paying at least the bulk of the proceeds to the deceased partner's estate and *not* use them to fund extra bonuses to the partner group. We believe it is in the best interest of the firm to use those proceeds to get that buyout liability off the books—pay it off. But that is also why we recommend a discount on the valuation of the retirement benefit to allow the firm to have enough money left over from the insurance proceeds to help cover some of the excess costs we've mentioned previously.

Policies Dealing With Disability

We also recommend that your succession plan address the disability of a partner. One policy that should be created should address total disability with another addressing partial disability. With respect to total disability, and in a fashion that's similar to the policy we suggest for a buyout at death, we take the perspective that if somebody leaves because of a disability, the compassionate thing to do is provide as great a benefit as possible to that departing partner. But from a business perspective, it's about balance and protecting the firm by making sure that the firm has enough resources to be able to pay off the disabled partner without putting the firm at risk. Therefore, we suggest similar discounts be applied to buyouts with respect to disabilities, as well (we will review some common discount combinations for death and disability in volume 2, chapter 16). Just as with a death, the firm will incur an opportunity cost when someone leaves unexpectedly due to a disability. The departing partner most likely will not have been able to take the time to do any transition work. The firm is most likely going to have to spread the disabled partner's work around as well as hire others to fill in the capacity gaps. This creates additional costs to the firm that need to be taken into account.

If your firm doesn't have policies that lay out exactly what the firm has committed to do under these circumstances, it is putting the individual partners and the firm in a lose-lose situation. We have seen partners go overboard being compassionate in these situations, yet because of what the disabled partner and his or her family is going through, even going overboard rarely seems like enough. Eventually, without upfront clarity regarding this topic, this terrible event will blow up in the firm's face despite possible herculean efforts on its part to take care of the disabled partner.

Just as with death, we recommend that you consider, depending on vesting, a discount in the range of 20 percent to 50 percent. Partners who haven't begun to vest would be vested at 100 percent, with a subsequent discount in benefits payable of maybe 40 percent to 50 percent. Partners who are partially or fully vested would be considered 100-percent vested but have a lesser discount of 20 percent to 25 percent applied to their potential benefits, for example.

Policies Dealing With Partial Disability

With partial disability of a partner, this process can easily become more complicated. What we often find with partial disability is that people tend to go in and out of disability over and over again. The problem is most firms don't have a way to deal with that in an effective manner.

We suggest that a firm's disability policy specify the number of months' pay that it covers initially—for example, 6 months, which is fairly common, depending on the disability policy with which it dovetails. But after that, if the partner is out (that is, incapable of performing his or her job for any 12 of 24 months), then the firm has the right to, and will, declare the partner disabled and remove that person as a partner. At that point, the partner will be covered under terms similar to those described previously for the total disability buyout. There are some nuances to how the disability policies and processes should work, which we will cover in more detail in volume 2, chapter 16, but generally speaking, it is important to understand that you can't run a firm effectively when you have a partner who is actively working for two months, out for four months, in for three more months, out for another four months, in for five months, then out for three months. Under these conditions, you can't manage the clients, you can't transition the clients, and you really are hamstrung about how to resolve staffing matters long-term unless you address how these tragic events will be handled clearly in your succession processes and policies.

In Conclusion

We suggest that your succession plan address these kinds of issues upfront and from the standpoint that you have a firm to sustain. One of the points we make with all of our clients is that we don't consult with a focus to protect the partners first, but rather the firm first and then the partners. Much of the discussion in this chapter sounds harsh, but when you consider that you have a business to run and other loyal partners and employees who count on this firm's viability, it makes sense to set up processes and policies that protect the firm first. As a board of directors, or as a partner group, you always can make exceptions, but we believe you ought to have a clear and equitable path developed upfront for addressing these heartbreaking events if they occur.

Conclusion

Factors to Keep in Mind

At the end of the day, we find that all too many firms don't have succession plans, and that those who do have succession plans rarely focus on enough factors to ensure that the plans will actually work. This is because the plans often are too focused on simply estimating when people are going to retire and whether the payment schedule will be manageable, while ignoring the most important aspects of succession management. We tend to get calls when a firm has prepared these schedules and finds one or more of the following events are expected to occur soon:

1. During any payment period, the projected outstanding retirement obligation for all retired partners will make up a considerable percentage of the firm's overall revenues, or the firm's annuals payments to partners will consume a prominent percentage of the firm's total profits otherwise available to pay partners.

2. There is no one in the firm who "can" or "wants to" do the work of the retiring partner, and the partners realize that the firm is obligated to pay for a retirement benefit with an insufficient annuity revenue stream to support it.

3. The partners realize that, in order to keep the annuity revenue streams that will cash flow the retiring partners' retirement benefits, the remaining partners will have to almost double the workload they are currently carrying, and they already are working at capacity.

4. Upon reflection on past retirements, the group realizes that the firm has been hurt by each previous retirement and decides that this is no longer an acceptable outcome; both the firm and the retired partner need to benefit from this change in status, rather than the partner benefiting to the detriment of the firm.

While there are many more scenarios that can motivate the partner group to reach out for assistance in the succession planning area, these are the most common. The good news is that what we have covered in this book addresses how we approach these concerns. When a firm implements these changes, the firm creates logical and reasonable protections to ensure its long-term viability.

The key to this process is to approach these discussions early enough that the conversations are about what is fair and reasonable to the firm rather than what is fair and reasonable to a particular partner. Once a partner is halfway out the door due to his or her pending retirement, these discussions quickly become personal in nature because these partners have already locked into an expectation. As you know from the topics we covered throughout this book, robust succession planning necessarily includes holding partners accountable for proper transitioning and other retirement-related conditions, with severe penalties assessed for lack of compliance with the process. These types of discussions would all sound like personal punishment from the perspective of a partner near retirement, and yet they would sound like good business practices to follow if the partner nearest to retirement were still four to five years away. Critical factors such as client and referral source transitioning, mandatory date of sale, damages for competing or otherwise harming the firm, as well as sensible vesting, valuation and payment terms, all need to be addressed in your discussions and ultimately recorded as part of the succession plan.

Probably the most critical part of a viable succession plan, one which our profession in general has been slow to embrace, is the robust, conscious development of people at all levels to ensure adequate bench strength for continued profitable growth and to ensure the capacity to pay out retirements as they occur. Based on our experience, the single change that creates the greatest leverage, flexibility, and probability of success for succession planning is the conscious development of a firm's people, from the top to the bottom. It is a best practice and something that should be number one on every firm's list of strategic priorities.

Other best practices include the installation and maintenance of accountability and compensation systems that facilitate holding partners and staff, especially partners, accountable to strategy, roles and responsibilities, policies, procedures, and budgets. In addition, continually looking at ways to add value to what the firm does for its clients while leaning out processes will be critical performance factors in the future.

Finally, as a firm's partner group looks out into the future, it is important to think through what sort of involvement and relationship the firm wants to maintain with partners who have retired or sold their ownership interests. Presently, most firms don't have a clear-cut approach to what roles and responsibilities that retired partners can acceptably fill will and won't be allowed. Unfortunately, this often results in partners who are being paid out for their retirement benefits while still managing client relationships and running a book of business. This is an untenable situation for the firm over the long term, and it needs to be addressed before it is too late. Working out these details at the last minute only puts the firm and the retiring partner at odds because the conversation is almost always interpreted as a personal affront to the retiring partner. Get ahead of this conflict. Paint a clear picture of life after the sale of ownership when the conversation could be about anyone rather than specifically about one retiring partner.

Developing Your Plan

This book and *Securing the Future, Volume 2: Implementing Your Firm's Succession Plan* are intended to serve as a comprehensive guide for firms to use as they identify the issues they need to address to create or improve their succession plans. As we use the term, a succession plan is not a full-color, 100-page manual, but rather, a working document with provisions and actions plans that are either outlined in the plan itself or contained in appropriate agreements, policies, processes, organizational charts, and so on that are referred to in the plan.

We recommend that you approach the development of your plan in the same order as we cover the material in this book. This approach allows you to build on each decision as you move through the process. This is the same order we employ to help our clients make changes that they previously were unable to do because each decision they make in an earlier chapter helps them make the necessary choices in later chapters.

We have made reference to a variety of supplementary and support materials in these books to help you and your partner group obtain an even more thorough understanding of the process and changes we are suggesting. Those materials include everything from CPE courses on our self-study learning management system, to our competency model and the related SIPA™ 360° assessment tool, to our Strategic Planning Virtual Facilitator for small firms, and more. We are providing you as our reader a discount on any of these offerings if they are of interest to you.

We wish you all the best in developing your plan! You may find the process to be frustrating at times. Just keep in mind that the work you are doing will help your firm become more sustainable as the efforts you make help you become more profitable and valuable at the same time.